TOWARD THE FUTURE

PIERRE TEILHARD DE CHARDIN

TOWARD THE FUTURE

TRANSLATED BY RENÉ HAGUE

A HELEN AND KURT WOLFF BOOK
HARCOURT BRACE JOVANOVICH
New York and London

The original French edition of this book was published in 1973 under the title *Les directions de l'avenir* by Editions du Seuil, Paris

Printed in the United States of America

Library of Congress Cataloging in Publication Data

Teilhard de Chardin, Pierre.
Toward the future.

"A Helen and Kurt Wolff book."
Translation of Les directions de l'avenir.
Includes index.
1.   Philosophy—Addresses, essays, lectures.
I.   Title.
B2430.T373D5713   1975   194   74-23802
ISBN 0-15-190910-5

First American edition 1975

B C D E

CONTENTS

FOREWORD

As a student of the phenomenon of man, Teilhard de Chardin constantly refused to see in reflective consciousness a mere epiphenomenon, a mere accident thrown up by nature, unrelated to the underlying structure of our universe. He was, on the contrary, at pains to integrate this 'redoubtable phenomenon which has revolutionized the earth and is commensurate with the world'[1] into the general structure of the world, and to disclose its origins, through the tentative gropings of evolution, in the very texture of primitive matter. In Teilhard's view, reflective consciousness was by no means what Professor Jacques Monod would have us believe, an anomaly or a secondary phenomenon in nature: it was a central phenomenon, revealing with peculiar clarity the mysterious forces contained in matter. With Sir John Eccles, the great brain specialist and 1963 Nobel Prize winner, he might well have said: 'My philosophical position is diametrically opposite to those who would relegate conscious experience to the meaningless role of an epiphenomenon.'[2]

There was another thing which fascinated Teilhard even more than did the origins and slow maturing of consciousness through the evolution of life: this was the contemporary spectacle of the manifestations of spirit within a mankind that has at last achieved maturity. Wherever he looked, he could

[1]*Christianity and Evolution* (Collins, London, and Harcourt Brace Jovanovich, New York, 1971), p. 105.
[2]*Facing Reality* (English Universities Press, London, 1972, and Springer Verlag, New York, 1970), p. 1.

7

see spirit at work; in every quarter, with unprecedented vigour and prodigality, a manifest rise of spirit was apparent in the unfolding of new ideas and the realization of new projects. Never, in its whole existence, had mankind known an age that could compare with ours. One had only to consider the progress in the fields of science and technology, the many determined attempts to create a juster and more peaceful society, or the richness and variety of all that the living arts contribute. Seen on the scale of the history of mankind, our own age appeared to Teilhard to constitute a real revolution. A new era, profoundly different from all that had gone before us, had just been inaugurated. The noosphere was beginning to disclose its true dimensions and to reveal its possibilities for the future. Spellbound, Teilhard set to work in an unflagging effort to understand this entrancing drama as it unfolded before him, and correctly to appraise all the manifestations of spirit – whether in the field of scientific research, or in the lines along which effort was being applied to the improvement of political and social structure, or, again, in the area of literary and artistic creation: and this both in the East and in the West, in the New World and in the Old. Everywhere the same drive could be seen, the same enthusiasm for work, everywhere one and the same hopeful expectation of progress and achievement.

Sooner or later, someone will have to undertake a study of Teilhard as a witness and observer of his own age. His essays and letters abound in interesting comments, with much valuable analysis of our present situation. His eye for reality, his openness to the life of his own time, his constant concern with historical movements show a characteristic side of his intellectual attitude. An endless list could be made of the events and tendencies whose meaning and significance he made

8

a real effort to understand: the First World War, the great
political currents of the twentieth century, fascism, nazism,
communism and the struggle for a true democracy, the
awakening of the Asiatic nations, China in particular (he fore-
told her rebirth and the part she was soon to play in world
affairs), and, most important of all, the great discoveries in
astronomy, astro-physics, nuclear physics and biology. We can
well imagine the enthusiasm with which Teilhard would have
welcomed the age of the first inter-planetary expeditions and
of the cracking of the genetic code had he but lived long
enough to witness them. His view of the future was based not
so much on study and interpretation of the past as on searching
analysis of the great changes that were being effected in contemporary mankind. All around him, he could detect the
symptoms that pointed to a 'rebound of evolution', and the
indications of a deep undertow which was sooner or later to
carry us to the full development of the 'super-mankind' whose
birth he foresaw.

It would be difficult to exaggerate the realist and factual
character of Teilhard's forecast of the future development of
the noosphere. Underlying all the events he studied, he dis-
cerned the same design and the same basic trend: progressive
unification of mankind, intensification of collective consciousness, birth of a socialized mankind, and, finally, movement
towards the convergent structure of evolution as it seeks out
its cosmic centre. Thus it is that spiritual energy, far from
coming to a halt or sinking back, is active in mankind, and is
continuing to evolve and to progress towards its full realization.

This new situation in which man found himself called for a
new attitude towards life on his part, a new moral philosophy.
Our traditional moral concepts originated from and were based

upon faith in a cosmic order which was accepted as stable and inviolable; it was a sacrosanct expression of the Creator's will, to which man had to submit unreservedly. Today, however, we see the universe in a very different light, not as a final, inevitable order, but as an order to be designed and created by man himself, for the purpose of his own fuller development. A moral philosophy based on the existence of a pre-existent natural order, serving as a model and a rule for man's activity, was meaningless except as part of a concept of the world which had permanently lost all validity. No moral philosophy was adapted to a forward-moving mankind which was puzzling out its road and trying to discover its true destiny, except one of effort, of achievement, of hazard and progress. The present crisis in moral attitude stems entirely from the fact that we have not yet grown accustomed to this new situation, and that we are not yet sufficiently clear-sighted and courageous to accept its consequences. In spite of our doubts and hesitations, this new concept of moral behaviour, based on man's responsibility in relation to his own destiny, will ultimately, and inevitably, have to be accepted; for it alone fits logically into the structure of our concept of the world.

Teilhard had a clear appreciation of this new situation. Not only was he fully aware of its importance, but he was anxious also to focus attention on all the consequences it entailed, and to make us alive to the changes it called for from us. Thus he distinguished two forms of humanism. The Middle Ages and the Renaissance had known a humanism of balance, which placed man's moral perfection in his conformity with the natural order of the world. Our own age had seen the birth of a new form of humanism: the humanism of achievement, which measured the value of a human life not by the degree of equilibrium it had succeeded in attaining, but rather by its contribution to the progress and spiritual growth of mankind. The humanism of balance had seen evil as refusal to adapt oneself to a pre-existing order; the humanism of achievement saw evil as refusal to contribute, according to one's capabilities, to the progress of mankind as it advances towards its true destiny.

In Teilhard's view, a similar transformation was becoming discernible in our concept of the Christian life. In the past, Christianity had been above all a religion of order. The fundamental question that Christians asked themselves had always been the same: what is the significance of Christ in a world which was created in a perfect order but has been upset by original sin? The answer was unambiguous: Christ had come to restore the order destroyed by sin, and to lead the world back to its primitive perfection. According to Teilhard, the fundamental question which the Christian of today asks himself is very different. Henceforth he must ask: what is the significance of Christ in an evolving world, at the heart of a mankind which is seeking for its future? A theology which started from such an expression of its fundamental question could not but lead to a new understanding of the Christian mystery. We know how Teilhard answered the question: for him, Christ had come into this world not to restore a primitive order which had never in fact existed, but to guide and invigorate the evolution of mankind by giving it its true centre and its true goal.

Thus Christianity became for Teilhard the religion of progress, the religion of evolution. Science teaches us about an evolution; Christianity teaches us about a 'super-evolution'.[3] Just as we needed a neo-humanism, so we needed a 'neo-

---

[3] *Christianity and Evolution*, p. 157.

Christianity', a Christianity freed at last from 'the slavery imposed on us by a certain group of accepted scholastic formulas',[4] a Christianity commensurate with the dimensions of our world. What we were living through in the Church was precisely, according to Teilhard, this slow but irresistible transformation of a religion of order into a religion of evolution and of progress. That was why, with all the vigour he could command, he called for the emergence of a new type of Christian, one freed from the strait-jacket of mediaeval theology, and now capable of fulfilling his real mission, which is the building-up of the world in Christ.

The essays contained in this volume of Teilhard's writings derive entirely from his eager concern to disclose the true meaning of our age and to arouse in us the 'sense of man and sense of the Christian' without which our lives cannot be lived with all the fullness of our time. That is why Teilhard will always be for us one of the great witnesses to this spiritual revolution which is now being effected, and whose manifestations, baffling and, indeed, distressing though they may sometimes appear, are nevertheless a continual source to us of boundless 'joy and hope'.

N. M. Wildiers
Docteur en Théologie

[4] *The Making of a Mind* (Collins, London, and Harper & Row, New York, 1965), p. 244.

THE SENSE OF MAN

'Non veni solvere sed adimplere.'[1]

THERE are 'events' in the human mass, just as there are in the world of organic matter, or in the crust of the earth, or in the stellar universe; and so there are also certain privileged beings who are present at and share in such events. It would have been possible for a witness, positioned further back in duration – provided his observation extended over a sufficiently long period – to watch the formation of our planet, the appearance of life, and the emergence of the human zoological type.

The purpose of what follows is to point out that we new-comers of the twentieth century are coinciding in time and place with a happening which is as massive as the initial forma-tion, vitalizing, and humanizing of the earth, and is developing at a tempo which keeps pace with our own experiences. This happening is the awakening of the sense of man, by which I mean that terrestrial thought is becoming conscious that it constitutes an organic whole, endowed with the power of growth, and both capable of and responsible for some future.

Such consciousness has not always existed; it has emerged only quite recently, and yet, even so soon after its dawn, its rays have so penetrated us that our whole interior life is now permanently impregnated by them. It is, one might say, cast in

[1] 'I have come not to abolish but to fulfil.' Matthew 5: 17.

a new mould. It is this event that I propose briefly to explain in this essay.

I. BEFORE THE AWAKENING OF THE SENSE OF MAN

There is no task more arduous for our mind (nor one that so soon calls for an effort beyond our powers) than to emerge from our own selves in order to meet the thought of those who are spiritually far removed from us. What could be the inner vision of a man for whom the earth was flat, the sky a convex bowl; for whom space had definite limits, and time was demarcated and homogeneous? Is there, then, anyone who could infuse himself, without distorting it, into the soul of an inhabitant of the ancient world, of a primitive man, or of a beast?

Today, we are so familiar with the ideas (whether properly understood or not) of progress, of the process of becoming, that we find it difficult not to include them among the essential ideas which provided the intellectual foundation on which Plato, Aristotle, or St Thomas built. If those great minds did not enlarge on matters that mean so much to us, the explanation, we might be inclined to say, is that they weighed them and found them beneath their notice.

Nevertheless, we find ourselves forced to accept the evidence of history. Although Aristotle, Plato, and St Thomas may well have been, individually, more powerful thinkers than any we could name today, yet not one of them saw the world as we now see it; and this because in their day the collective human-kind of which they formed a part was not yet ripe for such a vision. They had, of course, a certain perception of the solidarity of man and of the changes that take place in man. In their view, however, these changes have never amounted to more than accidental diversification or repetition of uniform cycles; nor was man's solidarity anything more to them than a theoretical or juridical bond. Until the eighteenth century (and even after it, indeed) and for Christian thought in particular, the fate of the individual (considered moreover almost exclusively in the 'supernatural' areas of his being) completely overshadowed the collective destinies of the whole. The affairs of men played a large part in the thinking of the theologians and moralists of yesterday, but (as is today still too often true) there was no room for the affair of man, and still less for the affair of the universe, *specifically as such*, and both involved as such in the creation.

We often delude ourselves by the belief that we do not differ mentally from the men of the century of Louis XIV. But can you imagine any modern man who could breathe freely under the burden of the world in which, for example, Bossuet's vast scope of thought was perfectly at home?

For Bossuet, an unexceptionable interpreter of his own generation, the visible world formed a completely unvarying framework, within which, until the end of time, man was to repeat himself, ever identical; and with no function other than to restore to God, by *intellectual obedience* and *temperance in their use*, the manifold objects which were harmoniously ordered once and for all by the Creation. It is the very concept to be found in the celebrated 'foundation' of the *Spiritual Exercises* of St Ignatius; and it is the idea which still persists today in the wording of the catechism: 'Man was created to know God, to serve and love him, and so to attain eternal life.'

But suppose we turn from Bossuet to any lay thinker you like of the seventeenth century, and question him. He will give us a different answer from that of the Christian doctor; yet even so, the view he has of the world as he looks around him is still, as it was for the great bishop, essentially individualistic and static. Man is nothing but a witness or a sojourner on earth, more or less observant and concerned as the case may be.

What is most characteristic of the static and fragmented picture that coloured collective human thinking only two centuries ago is the position accorded in those days, by believers no less than by unbelievers, to science and research. There was no lack, it is true, of scientists and students (nor, indeed, has there ever been since Icarus and Prometheus), who were already in some obscure way impelled by a deep-seated instinct for a sacred duty. But it would not appear that these men normally understood themselves correctly – and still less that they were correctly understood by others.

Until the eighteenth century, the scientist was primarily the enquirer; he was a man who was led by a harmless mania, or by his abundant leisure, to indulge in a respectable, interesting, but rather useless occupation. Inside the religious world, he became the apologist, whose delight it was to catalogue the wonders of creation, or who perhaps sought to refute opponents in some field of philosophy or scripture, or again perhaps hoped to adorn the Church with spoils won from the secular world. Nowhere was the serious student yet what we are now beginning to see him as: a sort of priest.[2]

A moving example of individual genius stifled by the collective mind of his own time was Pascal, who never broke through this constricting outlook. How can it be that a believer with such extraordinary gifts should have passed by the mystical treasures hidden in 'the effort to know' without

[2]Every work of discovery in the service of Christ, which thus hastens the growth of his mystical body, shares in his universal priesthood. (Ed.)

recognizing them? So close to us as he is in his religious self-questionings, how can a being so profoundly human be so far removed from us by his human faith? Pascal reproached himself for his scientific studies. He regarded the hours spent in physical and mathematical research as time wasted on useless trivialities. We need hardly say more to illustrate the revolution which in less than two centuries has destroyed the spiritual outlook we used to adopt towards the value of the world.

II. THE AWAKENING OF THE SENSE OF MAN

If we try to arrive at some sort of understanding of how the consciousness of man has developed in one hundred and fifty years, and thereby at the same time to determine more closely exactly where that consciousness is situated, we can, it seems to me, detect the simultaneous and convergent action of a number of factors; these appear to be independent, and yet the way in which they work together is most remarkable.

a. First, the influence of the natural sciences, and the discovery of time

Here, in what is perhaps the most important step, we have the basic foundation of the progress effected by human thought in all its history that is known to us. Until the middle of the eighteenth century, as we said earlier, there was hardly anybody who had any doubt but that the earth, its elements and its living beings, was a system of fixed things, in which the only element of growth was that of individual lives. In the world there was a time which was homogeneous and measured by the periodic movement of the stars. There were superficial distortions of sensible qualities and of states of soul. Deeper than these, but localized in time and place, there were also 'mutations of substance', chemical or of other sorts. And finally, there was the development of individual destinies. So far as change was concerned, that was all.

The great discovery of the natural scientists, since Buffon, came when they realized that we could speak of life, and of the earth, too, in terms of its age. Ever since that time, the universe ceased to constitute an invariable mass and structure. It was subject to a general movement (completely different from the old sequence that ran through the golden age, the iron age and so on), which carried it along, both in its totality and in its parts: and this movement was not local, but deep down in its very substance. Taken as one whole, the world was governed by a process of development, no less than any other organism. Mankind was confronted by things of which it could truthfully be said that they had a *past*, and with equal truth, therefore, a *future*.

b. *The influence of the physical sciences. Mastery of cosmic energies*

Parallel with the progress of the natural sciences, and even more rapid, there then came into play the advance of physics and chemistry. It has more than once been pointed out (and it is, indeed, a striking fact) that by about the end of the seventeenth century man was not much further advanced in his knowledge and mastery of cosmic energies than his cave-dwelling ancestors had been. He still had only fire with which to harness artificially the power needed for his social development. And then, in some scores of years, suddenly everything came in a rush: electricity, physical chemistry, radiations. It was as though a wide breach had been made in the energy reservoirs stored up by the world.

There is no need to emphasize here the vast consequences (whose influence is still far from being exhausted) that such an incursion of new forces entailed in the social sphere. What concerns us is to note the profound psychological changes it introduced into the fabric of human consciousness.

For the first time, perhaps, since his origins, man felt that he had real strength. After having been frightened of the elements, he thought that he might aspire to master them. His study of nature had opened up a vast expanse of time ahead of him, and at that very moment he found that the physical sciences had provided him with the power to use that future to its full capacity.

c. The influence of the social sciences. The mass coalescing of mankind

Man could not discover and master the forces of the world without recognizing that he himself was the most noble and the most formidable of the earth's energies. In fact, the short space of time (a mere century) which sufficed to get the physical and the natural sciences off the ground was distinguished by a vast labour of thought and research, applied by mankind to its own spiritual powers.

Man questioned himself about the dignity and the natural potentialities of his activity; and he realized that the group formed by the human race was still no more than a scattered and dormant mass. Ignorant and inactive, individuals were not extending themselves to the full extent of their powers; and, most important of all, the organized community, in which individual resources are meant to be accumulated – where they should provide mutual support, stimulating, we might say, a resonance in one another, with limitless intensity and sureness of purpose – this had not yet been constructed.

As so often happens, consciousness of this lack was simply the form taken by a deep-seated wish – or, to speak more accurately, it was the reflection of a vast movement towards solidarity which already existed in outline. Man began to feel the sprouting of his wings, and was wondering to what heights he might not fly.

Future ages, I am sure, will see the time in which we are living more and more clearly as marking both the end and the beginning of a world (the end of neolithic times, as has been well said, and the beginning of the industrial age). The importance of the changes introduced on earth by the coming of science will stand out with ever greater emphasis. But among so many great events, there is one phenomenon which, in the eyes of posterity, may well overshadow everything that has been discovered in radiation and electricity: and that is the permanent entry into operation, in our day, of inter-human affinities – the movement, irresistible and ever increasing in speed, which we can see for ourselves, welding peoples and individuals one to another, for all their recalcitrance, in a more sublime intoxication. It is the constitution, in progress at this very moment, of the organized human bloc, powerful and autonomous – the *mass coalescing* of mankind.

III. AFTER THE AWAKENING OF THE SENSE OF MAN. FAITH IN THE WORLD

And now, even though the movement is as yet only in its

infancy, we may say that it is born for all time. Whatever our reaction to it, it is here for good. After all the wild hysteria of the great revolution and the nineteenth century's often childish worship of progress, today, in the light shed by the discovery of time and of energies we have mastered, and of our vision of man's unity, we are *initiates*, and we are beginning to see into ourselves and ahead of ourselves, sharply and clearly.

In earlier days (one hundred and fifty years ago) we saw ourselves as passive and irresponsible spectators watching a great terrestrial panorama. We were still children.

Today, we have understood that we are workers pledged to a vast enterprise. We feel that we are living atoms in a universe that is under way. We have become adult.

There was a first occasion, it would appear – at the time of the Renaissance – when the sense of man tried to emerge; but the men who were then so entranced by the countenance of the world they had found again, misdirected their grasp. It was to enjoy nature that they reached out so eagerly; and everything fell to pieces in their hands. We, too, are experiencing a passionate re-birth into the universe; but we can see more clearly than did our ancestors, and our devotion to the universe is a devotion to a conquest to be won and a prize to be held. And this will be our salvation.[3]

It is only too true that there are many today who are still only vaguely aware of the new spirit which animates them. Nevertheless, this spirit surrounds them on all sides: and even if it does not make itself explicit in their speech, at least they can hear its voice – or, indeed, the judgement it passes on them. The airman who sacrifices his life in establishing an airmail

[3]And it is this, too, we may note, which makes our civilization so different in its essence from the ancient paganism of Greece, a comparison with which is sometimes suggested.

route; the climber who risks it in the conquest of Everest; the doctor who loses a limb by exposure to X-rays; all those, in short, who are today's pioneers of mankind are obedient, fundamentally, to the call to co-operate in a grand triumph which is greater than they. They tell us this in their wills, in their last words, and in their books.[4] And we understand what they mean – and anyone who does not understand loses our esteem. The moral support sought in the consciousness of forwarding the growth of the world by forwarding that of mankind *is tending to become a normal and habitual driving force behind every human activity.* What a fantastic change since the time of Pascal and Bossuet.

It is this realization that there is a solidarity of responsibilities and aspirations which properly constitutes the sense of man, and we would be justified in recognizing in it the psychological aspect, and therefore the experiential manifestation, of what we have called elsewhere 'the noosphere'. If mankind did not, physically and biologically, constitute a natural unit, provided with certain specific powers of organization, how could it produce a collective soul?

Let us, for the moment, leave the noosphere on one side, and confine ourselves to looking rather more deeply into the nature and the psychological import of the vast interior movement whose birth and first development we have just recognized. What precisely does the appearance of the sense of man represent in the history of thought on earth?

---

[4]To quote a few examples, taken at random: Younghusband's preface to the account of the assault on Everest; Professor R. A. Millikan's lectures at Yale University in 1928 on 'Evolution in Science and Religion'; the last testament of an American transcontinental airline pilot, quoted in the *National Geographic Magazine* in 1926; Drouin's dying words, 'The Atlantic, the Atlantic . . .'

The answer is inevitable: it cannot be anything but a power-ful phenomenon that belongs to the order of religion.

The nature of the sense of man is such that it brings men closer together, and inspires them, in the expectation of a future: in the certainty, that is to say, that something is becom-ing a reality whose existence is not strictly demonstrable but is nevertheless accepted with even more assurance than demon-stration and touch could afford. The sense of man is a faith.

Its nature, again, is such that it subordinates the whole of the activities for which it provides the basic directive force to the preparation and service of this great thing whose emergence is foreshadowed. The work now in progress in the universe, the mysterious final issue in which we are collaborating, is that 'greater unit' which must take precedence over everything, and to which everything must be sacrificed, if success is to be ours. The sense of man is a summons to renunciation.

Faith and renunciation – and what are those if not the two attributes essential to all worship?

It is perfectly true to say that what men are going through at this moment, in the incursion of the sense of man, is literally a profound conversion: the consequence of the revelation, through nature, of their situation and vocation in the universe.

Here we must proceed with caution, and not make the mistake of confusing what is happening with the emergence and dissemination of any one particular religion. The present event is much more massive than the coming of Buddhism or of Islam.[5] Today, it is not simply a matter of the special applica-tion to this or that divine being of man's religious powers. In us, at this very moment, it is the very religious power of the

[5]Christianity, too, constitutes a unique event, but by virtue of communication from above ('revelation') as well as by virtue of an awakening in the heart of man.

earth itself which is going through a final crisis – the crisis of its own discovery. In some very ancient human representations we seem to meet traces of the idea that to 'try to find out' is evil and forbidden by God. Later, the gospels might appear to have taught that every attempt to grow in stature, specifically as human, is vain.[6] But now the time has come when we look upon 'trying to find out' as the most sacred of duties. After beating against first this and then that restraining bank, man's need to worship has at last found the way out for which its troubled waters were seeking. At last it has explicitly recognized one of the essential attributes of the Messiah it awaited. We are beginning to understand, and we shall never forget, that in future the only religion possible for man is the religion which will teach him, *in the very first place*, to recognize, love, and serve with passion the universe of which he forms a part.

Admirable and mysterious self-reconciliation of life! At the very moment when man, dangerously armed with a more subtle mistrust, was beginning to call existence to account for the sufferings it inflicts upon him – at that precise moment the world (its discovery the very fruit of this new keenness of our critical regard) opens up for us the prospect of a future to which we cannot but submit. The awakening of the sense of man – itself brought about by the apparently fortuitous coincidence of steps taken independently of one another in the natural, physical and social sciences – is occurring at exactly the right

[6]Christ's message inevitably suffered from the limitation of knowledge at the time in which the sacred writers lived. In revealing himself, God raises the mind of man to a higher level, but has too much regard for it to substitute himself for it. Hence the necessity for a period of growth, in other words, of evolution. 'I have yet many things to say to you, but you cannot bear them now. When the Spirit of truth comes, he will guide you into all the truth' (John 16: 12-13). This guidance will last for the whole period referred to in the parable of the grain of mustard seed, i.e., from the sowing of the seed to the tree which covers the whole earth. (Ed.)

24

moment; just when it is needed to avert the terrible crisis of rejection and repugnance which would inevitably have shattered the thinking earth, had not that earth, *at the same time*, become conscious both of what was demanded of its activity and of the value of the universe.

Faith in the world has just been born. This, and this alone, can save the world from the hands of a mankind that is determined to destroy the universe if it cannot worship it.[7]

But what conflicts must it face before it succeeds in becoming established? And what support will it have to look for outside itself?

IV. THE CHRISTIAN CONFLICT AND THE RELIGION OF THE FUTURE

Faith in the world is irresistibly establishing itself at the heart of a civilization which is still dominated by, or which at any rate was formed by, faith in Christ. Inevitably, an extremely grave organic conflict is being produced between these two principles. If we appreciate the depth of this dramatic struggle, we have a perfectly clear explanation of the troubles which, for the last century, have been disturbing the world of established religions in the west.

a. The growing indifference of men to Christianity

A first fact which must strike every independent observer is the discredit which today attaches to the word Christian:

[7] Six years later, in 'Some reflexions on the conversion of the world' (*Science and Christ* (Collins, London, and Harper & Row, New York, 1968), p. 127), Teilhard strongly emphasized this point: 'I believe that the world will never be converted to Christianity's hopes of heaven, unless first Christianity is converted (that so it may divinize them) to the hopes of the earth.' (Ed.)

Christianity has become, in human terms, antipathetic. In earlier times it was feared or persecuted as being a power. Today, it is avoided, or kept at a distance, as a burden or encumbrance. That is the factual situation. It would be idle to explain this state of affairs as the result of ignorance or misrepresentation, for both those are effects rather than causes. The truth is that if Christianity has lost its attraction today, it is by no means because it is too difficult and too elevated (as its defenders pretend to believe) but for the contrary reason: in the form in which Christianity is generally presented today, its ideal is neither pure enough nor elevated enough. To our minds, the Christian religion seems narrow; and our hearts tell us that we cannot breathe in its atmosphere.

And the reason for this is precisely that Christianity has not yet allowed room for – gives, indeed, even the impression of being hostile to – the aspirations of the sense of man.

The sense of man believes in the magnificent future of the tangible world: and the gospel seems to despise it. The sense of man preaches enthusiasm and effort in the conquest of things: Christianity calls for indifference and renunciation. The sense of man discerns a universe emerging in radiance from the heart of the struggle for being: Christianity still confines us to the prospect of a fallen, static nature. There can be no doubt that between the gospel of certain preachers and theologians, and the sense of man, there is at present a deep rift. The temperament and structure of modern mankind is such that it believes in the world: a belief that, to judge by appearances, the Church of Christ rejects. The Church no longer gives the impression of 'feeling with mankind'. This is the basic reason for the atmosphere of hostility and indifference which surrounds her, even – indeed particularly – in the most progressive areas of society.

And this, too, is the explanation of the Church's present sterility. The proper mark of a true religion should be to spread like water or fire – irresistibly. If in these days the Church is making no headway, or can advance only with such difficulty, and that in the least active strata of the world, it is because something is lacking to the splendour of her truth; and that means that something is lacking to the fullness of her coincidence with the present needs of mankind.

b. The sickness of Christianity

If the appearance of the sense of man does indeed correspond, as we have said, to an organic (and in consequence an inevitable) modification of the fundamental religious capacity of man, then its effects cannot be limited to producing in unbelievers a certain loss of sensitivity to Christian influences. They must also be apparent in a serious disorder eating into the souls even of the faithful.

And this, surely, is exactly what we find everywhere around us.

Ask the Catholics you know: if they have any mental alertness and sincerity, most of them will recognize that, however faithful they may be in the practice of their religion, they do not find in it total justification for their lives. They give their adherence to Christianity: but *only for lack of anything better* – and provided that certain central points (relating to the value and origin of the world) be left discreetly in the background. This is no longer complete and ardent adherence to the light they have found. It is already (and how many have told me this) anxious expectation of a new gospel.

Nor could it be otherwise: however hard the Church may

try to keep believers warmly insulated in the cocoon of orthodoxy, she cannot prevent them from drawing from the common reservoir of human vigour the natural religious energy which feeds their 'supernatural' faith in God. As we have already seen, it is this primordial religious energy itself which is now being transformed as a result of the awakening of the sense of man. The Christian has no choice but to be carried along with the ground on which he stands, and thereby he escapes from the limitations of his own self. His eyes, and his heart, too, are changed. How, indeed, could he continue to find the same satisfaction and the same stimulus to his enthusiasm in the same representations and the same promises? He may, no doubt, try to persuade himself that he still believes in the prime importance of the Fall, of expiation, and of contempt for material things;[8] but he is already forcing himself, and even forcing himself out of true. There are ways of looking at things which we shall never again accept, because they have become alien to the soul of man. No one has ever been able to re-kindle a love that has been extinguished.

c. The official reaction

Never, since its first days, has the Church had reason to feel the threat of so deep an internal rift.

Hitherto, heresies and schisms had confined their attacks to the forms in which Christianity was presented. Never, even when the dangers were most serious, had the religious transcendence of the gospel message been questioned by any opponent; but today it is the essential moral value of Chris-

---

[8] A primacy of importance, moreover, which derives from a view in which there is more Jansenism than orthodoxy. Cf. John 1: 1-18 and Colossians 1: 15-19.

tianity, it is its capacity to perfect man, which is being challenged.

An instinct of self-preservation is proper to every organism; and it is a wholly predictable reaction of this instinct which accounts for the hostile attitude adopted, most unfortunately, by ecclesiastical authority when presented with the first outlines of what has become the modern world. Even, perhaps, before our world had become conscious of its own existence, authority could feel the advent of the rival who was gradually to halt its progress and eat away its power. For all her protestations and parade of sympathy, the official Church has never liked science: and this because she has always been suspicious of new elements that might disturb her peaceful dominance – and, moreover, because she has never looked to the tangible progress of the universe for anything of value. In fact, ever since the first indications of faith in progress and the unity of man, have not the clergy constantly sought to suppress it, to condemn it, and to ridicule it? More cleverly still, have they not tried to belittle it by affecting to see in it no more than the effect of a secularizing of, and so a retrograde departure from, the Christian ideal?

Let us be frank about this. Fundamentally, the Church has never understood, as we understand it, the fine pride of man, nor the sacred passion for enquiry, which are the two basic elements of modern thought. However specious the explanations that may be appended to it, Pius IX's Syllabus was an attempt to condemn all that is most solid in our present hopes. A world completely dominated by the Church – as the Church has shown herself to be from the Renaissance until our own day – and were such a domination humanly possible – would have acquired increased capabilities from the point of view of sensibility and charity; but it would have lost all power to attack and penetrate the real: a warning would have been posted along the whole front line telling the enquiring mind that everything had already been found.

Nevertheless, under the impulse of a higher vocation, man looked – and found; and wherever he perseveres in looking, there again he will find. Is it to be wondered at that after such an experience he should be tempted to lose some of his respect and love for the Church?

In a moment we shall be considering what can be done to correct this failure to understand on the part of churchmen who have not recognized in the growing faith in the world the most powerful summons to Christ ever to emerge from the earth.

Meanwhile, let us concentrate solely on the fact of this misunderstanding. By her reluctance to keep in step with mankind, which she should have led along new roads, the official Church has allowed an increasingly wide breach to open, since the coming of science, between herself and the life of the earth. She has given the impression of no longer sharing in the life of the world: and that is a mistake which it will take a long time to make good. So it is, now, that a great part of the world has lost confidence in her.

In order, then, to maintain her power, she clings to an antiquated apologetics. She claims that the historically established miracles of the gospels entail for men the intellectual and moral obligation to conform to her dogmas, *whatever may be the new demands of man's religious sense.*

Her effort is wasted: the facts of psychology deny all efficacy to this method of intellectual conversion and domination.

We now see that what gives a miracle its demonstrative force is that it is produced within, and assists, a movement that, *quite apart from that*, shows a capacity to justify the religious development of the earth. If you take away from Christianity its power to direct human activity and keep it on an even keel in the new courses to which its destiny commits it, then the raising of Lazarus has hardly more power to command our adherence than the wonder-working of Buddha or Mahomet.

d. *The salvation of the world*

The gospel tells us, *'Veritas liberabit vos'* – 'The truth will make you free.' It is useless to deny the facts; what we have to do is to understand them and control them.

We have just seen that, in a first and perhaps inevitable stage, the official Church made a vain attempt to block the road for the natural religion of effort and progress. Let us consider now whether there is a way of preserving at the same time – not by any artificial device, but in a real way – the sense of man and the spirit of Christianity: of preserving each, and of using each to preserve the other. A misdirected reaction has driven these two vital forces into mutually hostile camps. Are they not, rather, designed for mutual support and completion? In other words, surely there is a way of bringing together in natural alliance the hopes of heaven and the hope of earth, no longer as hostile forces but as rightly ordered energies.

If this is to be done, it is first and foremost essential that the fundamental Christian attitudes – detachment, resignation, charity, purity – be readjusted to modern religious needs.

Christian detachment is still too often advocated or understood as an attitude of indifference, suspicion, or contempt towards the realities of the earth. The world we know is but dust or slime, and *the less contact we have with it, the saintlier we shall be.* We have to replace this negative doctrine of renunciation by abstention with the positive idea of renunciation by 'devotion to the greater than self'. In itself, contact with matter most certainly does not defile the soul or drag it down: on the contrary, it feeds the soul and elevates it. For many centuries the Christian could be accepted as being one who professed contempt for the transient. Henceforth he must be recognized by an unrivalled devotion of his whole being to the creative power which is building up the world *'usque adhuc'* – to the very point at which we now stand – even in the spheres of the material and tangible. What must mark him out is an *unparalleled zeal for creation.* Formerly to be detached from the world could mean to desert the world. In future the phrase will mean to drive a road through the world, in other words to make a sustained effort in all domains – even in those so wrongly regarded as 'secular' – and so attain, make use of, and develop what is continually loftier, more distant, and greater in the universe.

Christian resignation has been too readily confused with a dangerously passive attitude, and with accepting a line of least resistance to evil. Indeed, has not one way of understanding Calvary inclined us to speak and act as though suffering were *directly* good and enjoyment *directly* evil? But what the faithful must now understand is that while suffering and death – in so far as they are cosmically inevitable – can become, through God's providence, marvellous instruments of spiritual fulfilment and union, in themselves they are both, none the less, hateful to the Creator. And in consequence, if our first duty is to develop the world, a second and no less binding commandment calls on us to fight to the bitter end against every form of diminution and pain.

The charity of the gospels has for long been identified with that of the good Samaritan, who picks up the victim, bandages him, and gives him such solace as he can. Surely there must be some way of giving this great virtue an even more generous and more active form? Beside the soldier who brings in his wounded comrade, there stands another whose devotion consists in pressing on with the attack without a moment's respite. Love of our neighbour would wither were it to lose that flower of compassion from which sprang the rich harvest of the Hospitallers and the nursing orders; but it needs to give itself a more solid structure in some passionate attachment to the collective work of the universe. We have not only to ease but to develop; not only to repair but to build. For our generation, love of mankind can have but one meaning, to devote oneself with all one's energies and all one's heart to man's effort.

A more passionate detachment, a more militant resignation, a more creative charity and, we must add, a purity more inspired to informed action; a humility with more pride in its subordination to the universe; a kindliness more animated by the spirit of conquest; a virtue less akin to weakness or mediocrity; a salvation more like the success of a universal enterprise than the rescue of an individual; a propagation of the faith more clearly distinguished from a sectarian proselytism – that is what we are all looking for if we are to feel that Christianity is on the scale of our new requirements. We can already hear it coming; and it will, in fact, come automatically, provided the sense of man and the sense of the Christian can produce in our hearts a vital mutual reaction of complete sincerity.

To the informed eye, is there not already a barely perceptible change of shade? Original sin is very gradually becoming, is it not, something more in the nature of a tough beginning than a fall? the Redemption more akin to a liberation than a sacrifice? the Cross more evocative of hard-won progress than of penitential expiation?

A collective *optimism*, realistic and courageous, *must without any doubt take the place of the pessimism and individualism whose exaggerated ideas of sin and personal salvation have gradually infiltrated and distorted the Christian spirit.*[9]

Unbelievers should not see in this a mere intellectual juggling – nor should conservative believers regard it as an illegitimate development of dogma.

It would be difficult, I know, to find in the letter of Scripture the precepts of an explicit gospel of human effort. That, however, is inevitable. Have the gospels anything to say about the modern industrial crisis; and is there anything in them that points to the reversal of the principles that govern 'obsolescence'? The awakening of the sense of man, if I have made myself clear, is a contemporary phenomenon, which has brought into the world something completely new. It would,

[9]Because of the change effected, as we have pointed out, in man's fundamental religious power, all modern religious literature, having been written either before the change occurred, or, if after it, without taking it into account, is to some degree outdated: not in the sense that it is false or useless, but in that it must accommodate itself to the *change of curve* experienced in recent times by the '*anima naturaliter christiana*', as a result of the emergence of the new dimension I have called the sense of man. We must recognize the situation frankly: it is not only the *Imitation of Christ*, but our interpretation of the gospel itself, to which this correction has to be applied. And the whole world insists that this be done. Let us, then, say so in so many words.

As a typical example of Christian pessimism, I may quote the latest encyclical (June 1928) on Reparation. In this the history of the world is presented as a long series of evils, in which all man can do is to express his horror and make expiation. The only answer the Church can give to present-day aspirations towards a great terrestrial task which must be carried forward is to lament the misfortune of the new age.

accordingly, be as absurd psychologically to assume its pre-existence in the minds of the apostles (and even in the human consciousness of Christ) as it would be to assume that of the internal combustion engine – or the English language. There are two things, and only two things, we have a right to ask for in Scripture and to claim for it, if its sacred character is to be retained. The first is that when the intellectual and moral principles contained in 'Revelation' are applied to the new curve followed by the human mind, they shall continue to operate with no distortion of the relationships which constitute the essential image of Christ and the Christian. And the second is that, in this new situation, Christ and the Christian faith shall continue to demand acceptance, not simply as being adaptable to the new development of the human mind but as being structurally necessary to it.

These two conditions appear to be satisfied in the prospect I am now trying to open up.

The Christian attitude can find new vigour and enrichment within, and indeed by means of, the human aspirations that have most recently come to the surface in the consciousness of man: of this we have just satisfied ourselves in our examination of the chief evangelical virtues.

The light of Christ, far from being eclipsed by the growing brilliance of the ideas of the future, of scientific research and of progress, is coming into prominence as the very central core destined to sustain their ardour: this is now a truth of which we can say with certainty that it will continue to become ever more dominant in modern apologetics.

The more man, under the impulse of the sense of the human, is entranced by the idea that he may expect some great outcome from carrying further even his 'secular' effort, the more will he

35

find that he must exalt the value of personalization and of the person, which is the supreme human work. The more, again, man becomes alive to the idea of 'the human function in the universe' and so attains a higher appreciation of the part played in the world by the forces of deliberate choice and consciousness, the more will he understand that the appearance on earth of reflective thought entails almost necessarily another 'reflection' to complete and balance it: after the reflection of the monad upon itself, the reflection of the whole upon the monad – in other words, a revelation. Finally, the more man becomes conscious of the high seriousness and the hazards of being, and is thereby led to question what rights the universe has over his freedom, the more unavoidable will he find this third conclusion – that if no tangible element can give him clear evidence of the intervention of a real term to the world (can *guarantee* him, that is, the existence of such a term) then no argument of his own individual reason, no agreement of other minds, however unanimous it be, can rid him of this doubt (which means the death, the physical death, of his activity and his essential zest for living): 'Does the world really provide the way out of which we dream? Are we not life's dupes?'

Thus, and for reasons that are built into the structure of our souls, we see how necessary is the objectivity of some contact with a God; not a long-delayed contact, and one confined to the individual, but one as old and all-embracing as the whole human entity, and made with a God conceived as the supreme centre of personalization. And this, we may conclude, is the final condition without which our present grand hopes for the earth will dissolve in abject disappointment.

Faith in the world can have no solidity without an answer given since time began by that which is promised to faith in the world. Those spheres of the universe which are endowed with thought cannot exist without a physical principle of *spiritual* coherence and energy. If the whole is to command our allegiance, it must have a heart: it must not be faceless. In the whole range of our experience, the only principle we can see which can give the sense of man its justification and its solidity, is a Christ to whom are attached both a concrete history and the attributes of divinity.

CONCLUSION

It is written in the gospel: '*Non veni solvere, sed adimplere*', 'I have come not to abolish but to fulfil.'

Whatever men may do to discover more sublime roads and develop new ideas, Christ must always, if he is to remain the same Christ, stand ahead of their progress. At every moment Christ, and he alone, must be able to give a sense of direction and a guarantee to the growing expectations of the modern world. It is Christ who gives fullness (*adimplet*) and who consummates. It will become ever more true that it is by that sign, *and by that sign alone*, that we shall recognize him.

Either Christ, Christ himself and he alone, is capable of safeguarding the human aspirations of our day – in which case we are ready to worship him with renewed fervour; or his growth is not keeping pace with the finest of our hopes – and in that case he no longer means anything to us.

Then, indeed, should Christ disappear, what will be left to us to justify and, in the last resort, to develop our zest for existence and life?

It is fundamental to the present crisis that the cause of Christianity and the cause of the world are inextricably linked.

The world would have no internal coherence were Christ not at hand to give it a centre and to consummate it. Christ, on the other hand, would not be divine if his spirit could not be recognized as underlying the processes which are even now re-creating the soul of the earth. It is only an extraordinary lack of faith that can have belittled, feared, or even condemned 'the spirit of today'. The awakening of the sense of man cannot be anything but the dawn of a new epiphany.

The time has come when this must be recognized. Today[10] the Church, drifting in a backwater of abstract theology, of a sacramentalism whose standard is quantity rather than quality, of over-refined piety, has lost contact with the real. The guidance provided by the clergy, and the interests of the faithful, are gradually being confined to a little artificial world of ritualism, of religious practices, of pious extravagancies, which is completely cut off from the true current of reality. The Eucharist, in particular, is tending to become a sort of object whose validity rests entirely in itself, and which absorbs religious activity instead of making it work as a leaven for the salvation of everything in the universe. It is here that we have taken the wrong road; and that is why the progress of Christian truth has, one might almost say, come to a halt.

Christianity will never cease to stagnate, will never begin once more to spread with the vigour of its early days, unless it makes up its mind to gear itself to the natural aspirations of the earth. Faith in Christ, a faith given vitality by man's faith (now born, and never to be lost) in some universal progress – faith in the world, a faith vindicated by the solid, exactly defined reality of Christ – the mutually supporting passion

---

[10]It should be remembered that this was written in 1929. Since that time, some Christians, in avoiding the danger noted, have gone to the other extreme. (Ed.)

for Christ and passion for the world – these are now emerging as the twin poles of the religion of the future.[11]

Indian Ocean, February–March, 1929

The text follows that of Père Jouve, editor of *Etudes*, revised and corrected by Père Teilhard. Where variations of wording have appeared in successive copies, we have given preference to one of the earliest typescripts, which used to be in the possession of Père Valensin.

---

[11]The greater part of the 'Catholic clerical body' now agrees in allowing a progressively more important part in the Christian life to human activities. In their view, however, this part is never more than an adjunct, an extra, an overflow of the supernatural life into the secular domain. We hold, on the contrary, that participation in man's work and aspirations is by no means of subsidiary importance as an instrument in the work of salvation: it is the basic psychological core on which in every man is built, or from which is born, faith in and the gift of self to the supernatural.

In spite of the concessions that have been made, there is still a complete contradiction between these two points of view.

THE ROAD OF THE WEST:
TO A NEW MYSTICISM

THE distressing spectacle of the multiplicity of the world and of its present state of disorder, which in the end forces us into an impassioned faith in the possibility of reducing that fragmentation to unity – in that lies the common source of the various philosophical currents, and the various attitudes to prayer, whose successive emergence, much more than the creation of any empire or the discovery of any energy, is the dominating event in human history.

Without mysticism, there can be no successful religion: and there can be no well-founded mysticism apart from faith in some unification of the universe.

The One and the Many: whence comes the fragmentation? and how can there be a return to unity? The increasing clarity with which this problem is seen, and the gradual approach to its solution, are a probable guide to the stages (some of which are still to come) of anthropogenesis.

From time to time, it is true, it is as though this tremendous germinal thrust were hibernating.

Under the influence of an *agnosticism*, wrongly regarded as scientific, which refuses to allow itself to know anything beyond continued identity with the past, the modern world has come to accept the question of the unity of being as one that cannot be answered and is therefore not worth asking; and so an attempt is made to disregard it.

Even more dangerous, because they offer a plausible substitute for an ideal, are the still popular positivist or aesthetic (as opposed to noetic) forms of pluralism. These have sought to do away with mysticism, or to supplant it, by teaching that fragmentation is of the essence of the universe. Incessantly, every individual and every moment of time represents a new culminating point: everything has always been, and will continue to be, multiple. This is the cult of this moment's ego – a principle of infinite dissociation logically posited as the core of moral science.

The modern world has examined all the possible outlets to its activity, except faith in unity. It seems permanently to have forgotten Buddha, Plato and Paul.

Experience, however, has shown the sterility of these attempts to secularize the world. They have introduced no organic order, and they have constructed nothing; nor, indeed, by definition could they seek to or have the power to do so. Their influence has spread, but it has been as a solvent spreads. They have not converted, but perverted, the earth. To convert means to contribute a soul.

And now, the world of man – bursting with a new exuberance of energies and desires – disappointed, and yet more than ready to accept a new form – feels all the pain and anxiety of the need for a spiritual orientation. Forced back to the initial sources of action, the world is looking for the essential idea and ideal which are biologically necessary to produce (in the root meaning of the word) unanimity.

It is looking for it: but would it not, so far from looking, even reject what it is offered, if it had not already discovered at least the *conditions* that must be satisfied by the divinity which, in anticipation, it worships?

The purpose of what follows is to show how, in continuity with (and at the same time in opposition to) ancient forms of mysticism (particularly Eastern), mankind of today, the child of Western science, is even now – for all its appearance of sceptical positivism – pursuing along a new road the persistent effort which since time began seems to have been driving life towards some plenifying unity.

I. THE ROAD OF THE EAST

If we are to believe the ethnologists, primitive man (in so far as we can recognize traces of him imprinted in the backward tribes of the earth) went through a phase of confusion in his infancy; it was a phase when he was mentally incapable of clear differentiation, and he could distinguish only imperfectly between activities on the one hand and things on the other. Attempts have been made to read into this vague feeling of an identity or fundamental solidarity in beings evidence or traces of an advanced degree of wisdom. It has been suggested that 'primitives' had already, naturally and without effort, reached the spiritual peaks to which we are so slowly climbing. This we cannot accept. Logically, and in actual fact, the divine virtue of unity appears in direct ratio with the differentiation of the multiple with which it is in contrast. We must have been brought clearly and forcefully up against the separateness and the antagonism of the cosmic elements before we can be enthralled by the feeling of their underlying solidarity and their anticipated confluence. Pre-logic (in so far as such a thing exists) can know only a pre-religion or a pre-mysticism.

The first current of true mysticism (that is to say, of a tendency towards universal union) of which traces are extant in recorded history, and whose influence can be traced right up to modern thought, is that which originated in India some five or ten centuries before the Christian era, and has for so many years made that country the religious pole of the earth.[1]

We do not know whether any historian has yet been able to determine what psychological or physiological antecedents, what refinements of culture or thought, are reflected (whether directly or as a reaction) in the formation of this mysterious 'cyclone' on the plains of the Ganges; but the results are still here for us to see: at a given moment, the finest portion of mankind reached a unanimity of belief in the essential unity of nature, a unity which could be achieved only by a *release of tension* in the universe.

'The multiplicity of beings and desires is no more than a bad dream, from which we must awake. We must suppress the effort to find knowledge and love, which means personalization, because it tends to give consistence to what is simply a mirage: and *thereby* (this is the key-word in the argument), as a *direct consequence* of the disappearance of plurality, we shall see the basic design of the picture emerge. When silence reigns, we shall hear the single note. Phenomena do not disclose the substance to us: they mask it.'

In over-simplified terms, this is the 'Eastern solution' of the perfect life, of the return, that is, to unity. For the Buddhist who drains himself away physically, as for the Brahmin who concentrates himself mentally, the opposition between the one and the many is like that of two planes which the eye cannot see without shifting from one to the other. Unity is achieved

[1]Nothing could be less mystical (in the sense in which the word is used here) than the older parts of the Bible. Jewish monotheism, in its beginnings at least, is much more anthropomorphic than 'cosmic'.

by denying and destroying the many. This is the idea which, in a number of different forms, has dominated Eastern wisdom, penetrating it as far as Japan. It was in this refined and pessimist solution of the world that the soul of Asia was born and found its expression.

In our own time, there would appear to have been a renascence of 'Buddhist' mysticism, even in Europe. It has even been suggested, and with some anxiety, that the monist serenity of the East might well convert the confused pluralism of the West.

In fact, however, this revival of theosophy and neo-Buddhism appears to be founded upon a vast misunderstanding. As we shall shortly be seeing, the modern world (for reasons even more cogent than those which had formerly influenced the East) indulged, in its turn, in the dream of discovering unity at the bottom of matter. In an excess of caution, Christianity was offering the world expressions of the one that were confined to juridical terms, emphasizing only its relation to the individual: and the world eagerly adopted the ancient formulas of Hindu pantheism, thinking that there it would find itself at home. However, in so doing it unconsciously attributed to them an entirely new meaning. The 'pantheist' mysticisms of the West, in their essence, respect the meaning of, and cultivate, the *real* values of the universe. Logically, on the other hand, these values no longer exist for the Eastern philosopher. The one stands not at the pole, but at the antipodes, of the experiential; and it is in consequence impossible to attribute to it any character or any determinant, even in an 'analogical' sense. It is impossible to conceive it at the infinitely extended term of any line of knowledge or action. The one is the mere negation of all that we call 'full'. If we are to attain this void, we must rid

44

ourselves (and this is all we need to do) of every concept, every image, every desire.

This is the total death of constructive activity: the fundamental emptiness of the experiential universe.

In strict logic, the Indian sage cannot concern himself with anything the life of the world has been, is, or will be. His European followers, I fear, are a long way from realizing this.

Such an outlook is so strange to us that the possibility of an ambiguity is forced upon our minds. Has there ever, *in fact*, been a single real worshipper of vacuity? Is it not simply that deep down beneath its words (which are the opposite of ours) and its actions (which may well have contradicted its fundamental intentions), the East had vaguely seen and was trying to pin down what we shall later be defining as 'the road of the West'? In other words, when the Buddhist is infatuated with that which contains nothing, does he differ essentially from us, when we aspire to that of which nothing can be predicated? For all the assurances of Eastern philosophers, this is a view we cannot but question.

Whatever may be the truth about that problem, which is a psychological one, what we call the 'Eastern' solution certainly exists *in theory*, and must be put forward here, if only in order to make plain the exact nature and originality of Western neo-mysticism. In the abstract we can conceive that man may pursue (what, in concrete fact, the East has perhaps literally exhausted itself in seeking) the unity of the world through direct suppression not only of the 'state of multiplicity' but of the multiple itself. Under the influence of the same universalist aspirations, it is in a diametrically opposite direction that the Western solution, or Western road, is now emerging.

II. THE ROAD OF THE WEST

In the eyes of the founders of Eastern metaphysics and mysticism, the tangible universe, from which the wise man had to free himself, formed a complex, glittering system of objects moving in a closed circle. Since the multiple, whether dream or reality, was irreparably fragmented, sanctity consisted in breaking the envelope of things and so escaping from them. In direct contradiction to this, the West's basic solution to the problem of the one and the many is to consider the experiential universe as formed from a linked whole of elements animated, throughout the whole of duration, by an at least potential movement of internal coalescence. On this hypothesis, if we wish to arrive at unity we must refrain from the barren and foolish effort to escape from things without freeing them at the same time as we free ourselves. We must not reject things: on the contrary, we must love them and hold fast to them in their essence – which is, if I may so put it, to yield, at the cost of great effort, to a forward and upward pull towards a common centre. *Understood in the good and true sense, the multiple is by nature convergent.* If it is to be reduced, it must not, therefore, be suppressed – it must be extended beyond itself. The divine light does not appear in the night artificially created inside ourselves; like a supreme and inextinguishable glow, it plays over the organic shimmer of the world. The fundamental note of the cosmos cannot be heard in absolute silence; it rises over the harmony of elementary vibrations. Heaven does not stand in opposition to earth: it is born from the conquest and transformation of earth.

God is reached, not by a draining away of self, but by

sublimation. Such, if we are not mistaken, is the great religious discovery of the new age.

To look anywhere for explicit formulation of this doctrine would, we must admit, be fruitless. No one has yet been at pains to set down this gospel in black and white. But do we need a book, when the truth can be read in the most profound needs and attitudes of a whole civilization? In fact, if we take due note, the point of view we have just set out is already so accepted and so built into our lives that it hardly needs explanation. It is this view which is coming to be adopted by all the living branches of modern religions, and to form the basis of their gradual convergence: a convergence of all, from Christianity (see below) to the new forms of Islam and Buddhism. And the reason for this agreement is as profound as it is simple. It is only in this prospect of union (and escape) through *convergence* that all the demands both of our aspirations and of the experiential world can find satisfaction and mutual assistance: and this with perfect ease, and with no loss or distortion.

The ancient religions of the East hardly noticed more in the experiential (that is, the multiple), and could hardly distinguish more, than the incoherent and mystifying aspects of its aimless and senseless turmoil: and that is why they were so ready to jettison it. The modern world, it is continually becoming more evident, was born, body and soul, from the discovery of the organic time of evolution. We are coming to see ever more clearly that the nebula of monads forms an ascending and contracting spiral. Flesh and spirit, each one of us is involved in a cosmogenesis which we can no longer regard with doubt or indifference.

For us, the history of the world unfolds as a significant act, instinct with the absolute and the divine, in which the spiritualizing activity of beings emerges as a sacred energy. There can no longer be any question, therefore, of setting up a simple opposition between one and multiple, between spirit and matter. Each must be sought out and worshipped through the other. Divine unity surmounts the plural by super-creation, not by substitution. Such is the road (*the only road* open to it) which Western life has already instinctively adopted, and to which it has irrevocably committed itself.

In the conflict introduced into the universe by the existence of the multiple, it would already be much to have found a way out which can satisfy the needs of the modern world. The crowning success, the fullness of salvation, is that for the Western mystic one and multiple, faith and experience, are not reconciled simply as two inert diagrams constructed to complete one another geometrically. The two terms combine, in reality, like two sources of energy whose coming together produces a mutual reaction; and this governs an upsurge of continually purer and higher life. In the Eastern picture, a similar psychological phenomenon can be produced: contempt for, and weariness of, the agitation of the cosmos drives the wise man towards Nirvana, and the appeal of Nirvana can in turn increase his repugnance for the agitation of the world: and this can continue to the extreme limits of ecstasy. Yet the whole of this process, in theory at least, is bound to take place in the *negation* of material things, of passions, of images, and to tend towards vacuity. Logically (and even though perhaps nine-tenths of modern theosophists deceive themselves by transposing our modern concepts into an ancient idiom) the Eastern saint must try not to *sublimate* the tangible real, but to *thin it down to nothing.*

48

What a melancholy and unrewarding occupation to offer as nourishment to the spiritual enthusiasms of a world!

From the Western point of view, the cycle takes on a completely different significance, and a completely different vigour. Western man is driven to the discovery and conquest of unity not only by his dissatisfaction with present disorders and shortcomings, but also by the immensely powerful attraction of the countless incipient perfections among which he moves.

The scattered charms of the universe give him a glimpse of the beauty that would unite them all in bringing them to their fullness, and his perception of this nascent beauty in the universe redoubles his admiration for the chosen, the 'elect' substance hidden in the elements of the world. Man's part, then, is to progress further in consistence by purifying and so extracting the positive essence of the multiple. The unity of the world rests on constructive work – work directed towards concentration and not release of tension. And the man who understands this, it is he who will know the intoxicating charm that comes not from vacuity but from plenitude.

Looking at modern Europe, to all appearances disillusioned and pleasure-seeking, one might fear that now mankind has reached a peak of complexity and power it may come to a halt, may stand undecided, may fade away, out of pure boredom with life. There will be no danger of anything like this if we are right in maintaining, as we have done, that in every quarter men are beginning to see that the turmoil of the universe is not an incoherent dream, but conceals and paves the way for a divine advent.

As we were saying earlier, it may be difficult, at the distance at which we stand from the first Hindu sages, to discern the causes which determined the appearance of their teachings and assisted their astonishing diffusion. In the case of the new faith in the West, the connection of events is perfectly clear. A passion – not simply a rejuvenated passion, but one that has taken on a completely new form – for the coming unity of the world provides the soul, which is biologically necessary: and this is at hand just when it is needed to maintain civilization in the modern form imposed on it by an irresistible evolution of social and individual consciousness. The concept of a 'unity of convergence' is *the only concept on which can be built the moral philosophy and religion of a universe based on scientific research and progress.* In virtue of that principle, no conversion (if one may use the word) will ever have such deep roots as that which is now being effected under the cloak of modern unbelief.

Hitherto men have been converted primarily with a view to individual needs and hopes, or by national or racial pressures. We are now for the first time witnessing the inauguration of a spiritual movement, intimately linked with the progress of the tangible world regarded as one whole: zest for unity in order to preserve the universal zest for action; a new faith conditioning a new mankind; one single soul for the whole surface of the earth.

Western mysticism (and in this lies the secret of its strength) is the first in which the subject is unquestionably no longer the human monad but the world. It is essentially 'catholic'; by that characteristic alone we could recognize that, in spite of certain appearances to the contrary, it is the legitimate daughter, or, to put it more exactly, the now-realized term and evolved expression of Christianity.

III. WESTERN MYSTICISM AND CHRISTIANITY

As Western mysticism has made its appearance as an extension
of Christianity, so too has the modern world, to which that
mysticism contributes a meaning and an ideal. Historically, one
preceded and encouraged the development of the other. One
passed into the other. But what of the cost? the long delays
before it could be paid? Did the flower not kill the stem? Does
the original Christian soul still survive truly in the soul of
modern religion?

It would appear to be difficult to question that, in a con-
siderable part of its early manifestations, Christianity appears
as an offshoot of Eastern mysticism. The importance accorded
to the Sermon on the Mount, which exalts what is weak in the
world – the summons to a renunciation which is uncommonly
like a direct escape from the useless or evil multiple – a theory
of religious perfection which colonized the deserts – all these
point to the conclusion that in its origins Christian thought to
some extent failed to free itself unequivocally from the rut of
Eastern tradition.[2] From another angle, if we look deeper into
things, we see that the gospel is based on a certain number of
fundamental affirmations, such as that of the resurrection of
the body; and that if the import of these affirmations is fully
developed, they lead directly to the Western concept of the
universe. Already, when St Justin speaks of the salvation of
matter, what he is doing is precisely to turn his back on
Buddha.

When we consider these contrasts, it would appear that

[2]In his complete and tenacious fidelity to the evangelical counsels, Teilhard constantly
resisted a pernicious interpretation of the gospel which would read into it an abandonment of the fight against evil and an endorsement of 'dolorism'. (Ed.)

the mystical history of the West might be described as a long attempt on the part of Christianity to recognize and separate within itself the two roads of spiritualization, the Eastern and the Western: *suppression or sublimation?* To divinize by sublimation – that was the side chosen, following the profound logic of the Incarnation, by the instinct of the nascent world. To divinize by suppression – it was in that oversimplified direction that the accustomed ways of the East exerted their pressure. Until our own day, the two currents can be recognized in the forms of expression adopted by the Christian world – if not in its fundamental, and correctly interpreted, attitude. Use and privation: Christ and the Baptist: attempts have been made to see in this duality two essential and reconcilable components of sanctity. In reality they are the remains of two incompatible attitudes. Men like St John of the Cross,[3] carried along by, and kept on a straight course by, the general movement of Christianity, have undoubtedly lived in practice a mysticism which can be reduced to the sublimation of creatures and their convergence in God. But the way in which they interpreted themselves – or others have interpreted them – is still distinctly 'Eastern'; and we should have the honesty to admit that, in this aspect of their sanctity, they are now alien to us. God does not emerge from the night; it is on the radiance of noon that he stands. Or, if we can speak of night at all in this context, it is a darkness which is the very excess of, or what we might call the reversed aspect of, our own light.

The time has undoubtedly come when clarity and simplicity must be introduced into Christian mysticism. In the very operation of its natural growth, the world has made its choice: God lies at the term of an effort to super-develop, not to

[3]And also, to some extent, the author of the *Imitation of Christ.*

constrict, the universe. If Christianity is to continue to live and be supreme, it must henceforth think and speak, unambiguously and exclusively, the language of the West: it must not resign itself passively, but attack; not ignore, but seek; not despise the tangible universe, but become enraptured by its contemplation and in its fulfilment.

I have dealt at length with this elsewhere (in the *Milieu Divin*). I am not offering you a road which will lead you in the end to any form of naturalism, or hedonism, or of pantheism. Far from it.

In the first place, if Christianity, in conformity with its nature and with the needs of modern mankind, is explicitly confined solely to the Western interpretation of the world, then it can and must retain intact (or even increase) its ascensional power of purification and detachment. Precisely in virtue of their capacity to converge upwards, the elements of the universe cannot be fully attained except by constantly forcing ourselves beyond them, towards ever more spiritual zones. So, just as the Eastern road, the Western road leads through asceticism to ecstasy. The Hindu saint closes in on himself and drains away his self in order to shake off his integument of matter; the Christian saint does so in order to transfigure matter and allow it to penetrate him ('super-indui' – to be 'super-enveloped'). The first seeks to isolate himself from the multiple, the second to concentrate and purify it. The oriental seeks to escape by abandoning time, space and self. The occidental emerges from the plural by carrying it with him. And of these two attitudes, *only the second is capable of expressing to the modern soul the truth, the power and the irresistible appeal of the Cross.*

What is more, frankly Westernized Christianity has no cause

to fear a dangerous monism. No doubt, this very idea that in and around us the unity of the cosmos is gradually coalescing at the term of a universal convergence produces an echo in the modern soul of the deep eternal music which has mesmerized all the pantheisms. But has there ever, by definition, been any true mysticism without some element of pantheism? 'And then,' says St Paul when speaking of the plenitude of the Incarnation, 'God will be all in all: *en pasi panta Theos*.' If Christianity is to remain true to itself as it is Westernized, only one condition, and that an essential one, must be fulfilled: to the maintenance of the primacy of *spirit* over matter (which, as we have seen, brings with it the renunciation of possession), must be added the primacy in the spiritual of the *personal*, which brings together at the same time the maximum differentiation of the elements and their maximum union. And does not this latter primacy, just as the former, derive precisely from the nature and mechanism of 'convergence'? How could the multiple *be lost* in unity (which is what false pantheism consists in), when the ontological process of convergence which unites the elements is precisely the process which at a lower level makes each one of them incommunicably itself?

In short, as things stand now, if Christianity is to remain itself, it must come to the rescue of Western mysticism, and in so doing take it to itself. Left to themselves, the new wise men of the West might well relax in the enjoyment of what they have won. They would probably limit their hopes to the temporal and spatial horizons of the present world, without realizing that this limitation to an inferior and declining state of matter must logically destroy their passion for research and the vigour of their optimism.

In any case, they would lack the culmination which is almost essential to the validity of their outlook: an historical design, a name, and a face, to attach to the term of universal convergence. As the present metamorphosis of man's religious sense develops, nothing is as yet at hand to replace Christ in his role of the centre 'in whom all things find the consistence of their being'. Christ is still the only cosmic element we can see that can – leaving aside any illuminism or idle dream – give a body to modern hopes for a spiritual organization of the world. More, however, is still needed: the Church must recapture the visions so passionately described by St Paul, and must make up her mind finally to recognize and proclaim Christ, *the whole and entire Christ*, as fulfilling that role, radiant with the hopes and energies of the universe.

But to continue: mankind has now reached such a degree of concentration and moral tension that it can no longer postpone taking the spiritual step which will give it a soul. Agnosticism and pluralism are either dead or impotent. It is only a renewed faith in some unity to be born of the world that can preserve our zest for life. And at this precise point we come to a parting of the ways; to one side runs the ancient path of the East, away from matter, towards the minimum of questioning, of concern, of external effort – the unity which is disclosed with the negation of the multiple: and on the other side runs the new highway of the West, following a straight line to the mysteries of the earth, to the sustenance it provides, to the unity absorbed in domination of the multiple.

There can be no hesitation; and, what is more, the choice has already, to all intents and purposes, been made long since. History and experience both insist that it is in the Western direction that we must guide the progress of life. We must know more, and we must be masters of more, so that we may be more completely assumed by God. At the dawn of human kind, such an ambition might have seemed reprehensible, when the first energies unleased were rounding on the daring spirits who had released them. It might have seemed superfluous to the first Christians, when the physical universe seemed to have neither a past nor a future. But now that we have understood the importance of the work which is being carried on through the medium of our lives, it has become for us the finest expression of moral duty and worship. Both outside and inside Christianity, it is on this new gospel of masterful spirituality that the old world now parts company with the new.

Individuals, nations, races and religions, everything will disappear tomorrow which has not today hazarded its soul on the road of the West.

APPENDIX. THE TWO FORMS OF UNITY, AND THE MEANING OF THE MULTIPLE

As philosophers have long remarked, there are two converse notions of unity: first, unity by impoverishment, by taking away, or return to the homogeneous; and secondly, the unity of richness, by concentration of what is positive in determinants and qualities. The 'ens ut sic' and the 'ens a se'. Ether and spirit. Eastern and Western mysticism are simply the religious pursuit of the divine in one or other of these two directions – another way of emphasizing the reason for preferring the second to the first.

Nevertheless, there is an essential element in Western mysticism which is not properly brought out by simply relating it to the cut and dried system of two types of unity, the unities of simplicity and of complexity.

From the modern point of view, which is governed by the idea of evolution, the one is not merely opposed to the multiple as a total perfection opposed to a sum of imperfections: partially at least, it *is born* from that multiple. Its unity is, to some degree, *woven* from the plurality whose consummation and synthesis it ensures. And in this lies the *fundamental reason* as regards human activity, for *impassioned abandonment to effort*; what we do ensures, on the scale of the element, the unification of the universe. *It calls for nothing less than consciousness of this responsibility, and for nothing more, to make life of real concern to us.*

From this notion of the *evolutive structure* of universal unity (of the 'pleroma', St Paul would have said) is derived an extremely well-defined and encouraging significance to be attached to matter.

In the mystical or metaphysical systems belonging to the Eastern current, some idea of evil is always associated with the origin of the multiple: a dream, disturbing the initial serenity of essence, or a revolt entailing the degradation of some portion of spirit into matter. The plural, which should have been suppressed, must be evil by nature or accidentally perverted in its origin.

When, on the other hand, we admit the idea of a genesis or a fulfilment of the one from the elements of the world, these elements still remain, it is true, the source of all sin and all suffering – because of their temporary condition of disorder, itself the inevitable consequence of the still continuing process of attaining their union – but they no longer need a prior evil to explain their appearance and their initial distribution. They are no longer the shattered fragments of the amphora, but the dust of the elemental clay. The multiple is not a secondary waste product; it exists, quite simply, because it is necessary for a certain fulfilment of unity. It is, in the most fundamental sense, the positive and essential condition of an absolute progress. *The idea of a congenital flaw in matter can now be seen to be as incompatible with Western mysticism as its absolute contingence.*

Seen in this way, the idea we are now coming to form of the structure and function of matter is closely linked with Christian views on the final consummation of the universe. On the one hand, in virtue of the Incarnation, God can no longer (at least *hic et nunc* and for ever) dispense with the multiple into which he once entered; and on the other hand, the real entity 'God+multiple' in Christo Jesu, seems, both in Christian practice and in Pauline mysticism, to represent a perfection which, however qualified it may be as extrinsic to God, introduces with itself a real completion into the equilibrium of universal being.

Here we find implicitly the concept of the multiple as fundamentally good, and to some degree necessary. As follows from what we were saying earlier, Christianity is in an excellent position to rescue the hesitant steps of Western mysticism and lead them along an exact, well-tried, and direct line. It is the only guide at hand to pilot us along the road of the West.

But here again, we should note, we who are of the faith must make up our minds to a partial but far-reaching revision of our views on the origin and evolution of the universe. Precisely as in the case of asceticism and mysticism, we still seem to find in Christian representations of cosmogony a certain cross-infection between Eastern and Western views. Although St Paul combined them into a single picture, the ideas of a first creation (absolutely contingent, and hence hardly explicable) and then of a general fall (equally contingent, and hence a poor reflection of the Creator's glory) do not fit in well with those of an Incarnation which culminates in a sort of mutual plenifying of the one and the multiple. In the complete concept we can trace the mixture of elements borrowed from judgements of value or principles of solution that are very different or even contradictory. To separate these elements, and then to select from them, and so arrive ultimately at a Christian cosmogony with no limits to its horizons and no taint in its structure – one worthy of the universal Christ who is its crowning glory – this is a task that cannot be postponed.[4]

Penang, 8 September 1932

[4]In order to follow the writer's spiritual journeying, it is essential to re-read the essay which provides his starting point, and which he called 'an introduction to mysticism' (*Writings in Time of War*, Collins, London, and Harper & Row, New York, 1968, pp. 115–49). (Ed.)

THE EVOLUTION OF CHASTITY

EVER since religions have existed, they have always tended to express themselves, in the most sublime of their manifestations, in the form of chastity; and this is as true of Buddhism as it is of Christianity. We always find that for the complete initiates, the *perfecti*, victory over sexual attraction is ultimately the supreme mark of the triumph of spirit.

I shall not try here to contest, but rather to justify the profound value of this reaction. In its spontaneity and its universality, the call to chastity seems to me to be too intimately derived from life's infallible instincts for it to be possible to regard it as a value with which we can now dispense.

At the same time I believe it to be true of this, as it is of so many other matters, that we are still a long way from having accurately determined the nature of what we undoubtedly feel. Consciousness, we know, does no more than grope its way forward, one approximation following upon another. Hidden beneath the idea of virginity there lies, I am sure, a precious, significant and active element; but I am no less sure that no formulation of that idea has yet been found which is satisfactory either in theory or in practice. The doubt originated from my own personal experience, and has been magnified by the increasing number of elevated and sincere minds who no longer see anything fine in the restrictions of asceticism.

It is now only a blurred image of chastity that is projected on our physical and moral universe. It is constantly either expressed in obsolete language and systems – or justified by a complex of disparate reasons, many of which no longer have the power to move us. What we have to do is to define precisely what constitutes the excellence of chastity; and in order to do that we must relate it clearly to the structure and values of the modern world.

It is this that I have had in mind when writing what follows.[1]

I. THE EMPIRICISM OF THE CHRISTIAN
APPROACH TO CHASTITY

Just as, and by the very fact that, Christianity is today the most progressive form of religion, so, and by that same fact, it is to Christianity that we should look for the most highly developed expression of the doctrine of chastity.

In these days, this doctrine (or rather, as I shall be explaining, this *practice*) is very clearly summed up in the two following injunctions:

1. The union of the sexes is good, and even holy – but *exclusively* for the purpose of reproduction.

2. Apart from that purpose, any intimacy of union between the sexes must be reduced *to the minimum*. The moral ideal (higher even than marriage) is virginity.

[1] It may be easier to follow the author's argument more clearly, as he develops it in the text, if it is summarized as follows:

Père Teilhard sets out to define the essence of virginity, in the light of the problems he meets in his own environment. In order to do so he:

a. begins by ruling out obsolete concepts, such as the Manichaean concept of the impurity of matter, which entailed an ideal of virtue based on detachment;

b. moving then to the dynamic aspect, he asks: is human love, as some maintain, an energy of the highest rating in spiritualization? Or, 'are we not burning up in human love some part of what is absolute in us?';

c. turning finally to the sense of evolution in man, he concludes: 'Love is undergoing a process of change within the noosphere, and it is in this new direction' (the direct drive towards its creator) 'that the collective transition of mankind into God is being made ready.' (Ed.)

These two rules cover satisfactorily the majority of cases; and for some centuries they have been successful in assuring the two essential human functions of 'propagation of the species' and 'spiritualization'. Nevertheless they are by no means compatible – they are complementary in practice rather than logically connected. Prudent and comprehensive though they are, yet we can detect opposition between two incompletely reconciled points of view.

This arises from the fact that, in the sphere of sex, what we have is not exactly a developed theory, but simply a *Christian empiricism*. Open any book you choose of moral theology or ascetics. What guidance do we find in it for the use of our senses? Categorical rules? Yes. Explanation? No. Apart from a few isolated, and generally fanciful attempts, there has been no systematic examination of the 'formal effect' of the 'saintly virtue'. On the other hand, a very elaborate and very psychologically aware code is developed, of rules, methods and counsels – based on the traditional practice of the saints, and ultimately on a very small number of gospel texts. And that is all.

This 'empirical' character, we should note, is by no means a mark of biological inferiority. Far from it. The more widely a reality is seen to be based on a development and an achievement that is experiential in nature, the better its chances of proving fruitful and definitive: but only *provided we try to intellectualize it.*[2]

What, then, are the elements – emotional or rational – which we can recognize as the basis of Christianity's cult of chastity? A whole series of them can, I believe, be distinguished, differing

---

[2]Intellectualize means in this context to justify theoretically the value of a procedure that is otherwise entirely 'empirical'. (Ed.)

quite considerably, either according to the motives they bring into operation or according to the stage of moral evolution they represent.

In the first place, and most fundamental of all, we can detect a *physiological presupposition* which colours more completely than one would imagine the whole development of Christian thought in connection with the Fall, sanctification, and grace. By this I mean the idea – though 'impression' would be the better word – that sexual relations are tainted by some degradation or defilement. By the material conditions of its act; by the physical transports it entails; by a sort of clouding of personality that accompanies it – 'passion', man instinctively feels, has about it something of animality, of shame, of fever, of stupefaction, of fear, of mystery. Here we meet, in its most basic and most insistent form, and at its most acute, the *whole* intellectual and moral *problem of matter*. Sexuality is sinful. Later, we shall try to determine how much of this primitive 'horror' can and should be retained. The point that matters now is that its influence, a heritage from Judaism, has passed into the Christian concept of chastity – and that in spite of the sanctity accorded to marriage. '*Hi sunt qui cum mulieribus non sunt coinquinati.*'[3]

After the physiological element comes the *social element*. It would be a distortion of the religious phenomenon to reduce it to an organ of defence directed by the group against the individual; but without that collective function, too, something would be lacking to religion. For what is more important to society than maintenance and control of man's powers of reproduction? In these matters, strict policing is needed to establish the best system and to defend it against those who

[3]'It is these who have not defiled themselves with women.' Revelation 14: 4.

would abuse it. This concern for 'public safety' does much to explain in Christianity the load of penalties and threats, the stigma, attached to misdemeanours of the flesh – as it explains, too, the wealth of praise lavished on chastity. With fire lurking in the human edifice, it is *safer* to flood the whole premises.

This is social tutiorism.[4] But there is *individual tutiorism*, too. It is probably for lack of some compensating idea to balance the exaggeration that Christianity has developed in itself, to the point of what a biologist would call hypertrophy, the ideas of guilt and damnation. The one thing that matters for the soul is to save *itself*, and to do so *by absence of sin*. From this arises a whole system of restrictive asceticism in relation to sexuality. To avoid any risk of vertigo, one has to stay as far as possible on the safe side of the cliff – one has to run away. In order not to give way to the blandishments of pleasure, in order not to be carried away by enjoyment, one has to cut away the very roots of pleasure and inflict pain on oneself: privation and penance.

This practice is in itself largely defensible. It contains the elements of a valuable prophylactic. What is more disturbing is to see it gradually transformed into a practical system, in which an *absolute* sanctifying quality is implicitly accorded to suffering and sacrifice. This odd inversion[5] of natural values to all intents and purposes endorses the value of chastity conceived as a moral castration – and it has opened the door to all the extravagances of penitentialism. However – and this is to the credit of the gospel – this asceticism is justified for Christians only in so far as it develops ultimately into a refined mysticism.

[4]Tutiorism consists in adopting, when in doubt, the solution which involves the least risk. Some theologians or spiritual advisers have made it a rule of virtue. (Ed.)
[5]This inversion turns pain, the normal symptom of effort, into a result which, it is held, is of value quite independently of the result to which the effort is directed.

If the real believer nurses so apprehensive a love for the restrictive practices of chastity, it is because he sees in them the necessary means of preserving the flower of his charity. And this comes about as follows.

For every religion worthy of the name, to worship means to lose oneself unitively in God. In Christianity, however, this union of the divine takes on a precisely defined meaning: it comes into effect as a supreme marriage. The saintly soul is in some way Christ's bride. As a consequence of this fundamental concept, Christianity's empirical approach to chastity – and herein lie both its strength and its weakness – develops as an extension to man-God relationships of the ideal code accepted between earthly lovers: hence physical virginity. But most of all, and even more clearly, a holding-back of the powers that love commands. It is the heart that dictates chastity. We have been moving hitherto in the half-dark of physiology, and now at last we find a fully human clarity. Christian chastity is ultimately a *transposition into religion of the lover's fidelity*.

It is, then, the notion of fidelity that we shall be chiefly concerned to examine more fully when we come to discuss the supremely nice question of an evolution of chastity. Here we may simply note that, in conformity with a restrictive and penitential asceticism, Judaeo-oriental in tone, the Christian expression of this fidelity has so far been primarily in terms of privations; so much so that the whole theory of Christian sanctification – based, and rightly based, on sublimation of love – tends to culminate in a sort of *separatist view of matter*.

True Christianity has never condemned matter, but has, on the contrary, constantly defended it against monist or Manichaean heretics. Christianity draws nourishment from sacramental practices, and lives in the hope of a resurrection. Yet this care for the body is combined with an odd mistrust of the earth's resources. Creatures are good: and yet they are not good. The world might well have been created as we see it: and yet it contains within itself a hidden perversion. And so once more we come up against the complexity of the still insufficiently intellectualized notion of the original Fall.

In this somewhat ambiguous situation, the Christian's rule will be (as the book of the *Imitation* says) to take less rather than more. He will save his body by losing it. He will sublimate matter by attenuating it. The flesh does not form an atmosphere or a nebula around his spiritual self, but *a duplicate*. For reasons that we cannot understand, this satellite, mysteriously associated by the Creator with the spirit, is inconstant and dangerous. Above all, it is wilful. We must hold it in subjection, even when ministering to it.

Logically, the saint will attain the maximum of self-perfection by a *minimum* use of matter – and, most particularly, of matter in its most virulent form: the feminine.

II. A NEW MORAL CONCEPTION OF MATTER

It is thus that Christianity has carried further than any other religion the practice of chastity, of which it has developed the most perfect type in the figure, so lovingly cultivated and for so many centuries, of the Virgin Mary. And today it is Christianity that constitutes the surest defence of chastity and its richest storehouse.

Nevertheless, it by no means follows that the ideal of virtue which it conserves and seeks to make more widely accepted, still retains for our modern minds the vigour and precision of its first magnetic charm. The moral value of chastity (or at least the traditional interpretation and discipline), long accepted almost without question, was seriously challenged by the Reformation, and for many of us is now coming to lose its obvious rightness. Nor should this phenomenon be attributed, by oversimplification, to human perversity, and, in consequence, be underestimated. It must be faced conscientiously and straightforwardly; for, in a number of aspects, it is far from behaving as a retrograde movement – it is manifesting itself, rather, as an attraction exerted by a loftier ideal.

Underlying the modern mind's objection to the gospel code of purity, and running deeper than any pagan libertarian thought, we can distinguish, I believe, a re-awakening of the religion of spirit. On the one hand, the whole physiological and social side of chastity is again being challenged: the importance of virginity or material integrity of the body has become as unintelligible to us as respect for a taboo. And on the other hand, for reasons which we shall try to analyse later, we are finding a successful venture into experience more attractive than preservation of innocence; we now estimate the moral value of actions by the spiritual impulse they provide.

In its extreme form, disregard for the material side of chastity is expressed in a radical, and ingenuous, solution. 'In short,' we often hear, 'sexuality has no significance at all from the moral and religious point of view: you might as well speak of running your digestion on moral principles. So far as his sexual side is concerned, man must no doubt have a care for health, and exercise temperance. A controlled use will give him balance and an added zest for action. But by no stretch of imagination can we agree that physical chastity has anything to do with spiritual virtue. There is no direct relationship between sanctity and sexuality.'

I cannot accept this idea that two independent variables, 'spirit' and 'matter', operate in the domain of moral growth. It is not in conformity either with the deep instinct which has always made men suspect that something more valuable than mere self-control underlies chastity – or, quite simply, with the all-embracing laws of biological development. Moreover, the idea itself is no more than an elementary form of impatience, a mere gesture, produced as part of the reaction which makes the modern mind question the pre-eminence of chastity. There is another idea which seems to me to be much more connected with the basic evolution of our thought. This (the most important basis of psychoanalysis) is that the energy which fuels our interior life and determines its fabric is in its primitive roots of a passionate nature. Like every other animal, man is essentially a tendency towards union that brings mutual completion; he is a capacity for loving, as Plato said long ago. It is from this primordial impulse that the luxuriant complexity of intellectual and emotional life develops and becomes more intense and diverse. For all their height and the breadth of their span, our spiritual ramifications have their roots deep in the corporeal. It is from man's storehouse of passion that the warmth and light of his soul arise, transfigured. It is there, initially, that we hold concentrated, as in a seed, the finest essence, the most delicately adjusted spring, governing all spiritual development.

When we have finally weighed things up, it is apparent that only spirit is worth our pursuit; but deep within us there exists a system of linkages, both sensitive and profound, between spirit and matter. It is not only that the one, as the Christian moralists say, supports the other: it is *born* of the other, and so we should not simply say, 'To lighten the burden of the body, be abstemious', but, 'To maintain the drive of spirit, fill up with fuel.' *Underlying the religion (or moral science) of spirit, a new moral conception of matter is asserting itself.*[6]

The idea that there is a universal genesis of spirit through matter (the idea, in other words, of a spiritual power of matter) has origins which outflank the problem of chastity. It arises from that vast experience of mankind which, in the course of a century, has given a completely new picture of the world: the discovery of universal time and evolution. Until the eighteenth century, or thereabouts, the debate about the principles of moral science was confined to two very simply distinguished groups: the spiritual and the material. The latter claimed that the business of life was to enjoy nature as they found it. The former urged that we must, on the contrary, hasten to shake off the dust of material things. Both, however, agreed in admitting implicitly that the world had never moved – or, at any rate, had come to a final halt. It was then that through all the channels of thought and experience there entered into us the consciousness that the 'universe around us' was still functioning as a vast reservoir of vital potentialities. It used to be believed that matter was either stabilized or spent; and it was found to be inexhaustibly rich in new psychological energies. It used to be thought that nothing essential was still left to be discovered; and now we realize that everything is still waiting to be found. The *perfecti* came uncommonly close to rejecting the world like a squeezed lemon: we shudder at the idea of that wasteful gesture, which would have brought to a dead stop the conception, still being developed, of spirit. Then we revised other judgements of value in the light of this

[6]The author, it will be observed, has transcended the opposition between matter and spirit which is incompatible with human unity. (Ed.)

discovery, and found that the transformation of our intellectual views on matter was gradually, both in fact and logically, invading the domain of our affective and emotional life. Woman is, for man, the symbol and personification of all the fulfilments we look for from the universe. The theoretical and practical problem of the attainment of knowledge has found its natural 'climate' in the problem of the sublimation of love. *At the term of the spiritual power of matter, lies the spiritual power of the flesh and of the feminine.*

It is here, if I am not mistaken, that we reach the source of the divergence which seems to detach our modern sympathies from the traditional cult of chastity. The Christian code of virtue seems to be based on the presupposition that woman is for man essentially an instrument of generation. Either woman exists for the propagation of the race – or woman has no place at all: such is the dilemma put forward by the moralists. All that is most dear to us in our experiences, and most certain, revolts against this simplification. However fundamental woman's maternity may be, it is almost nothing in comparison with her spiritual fertility. Woman brings fullness of being, sensibility, and self-revelation to the man who has loved her. The truth is as old as man himself; but it could not take on its full value until the world had reached such a degree of psychological consciousness that, for a human race that had spread far and wide and had a sound economic footing, the problems of food supplies and of reproduction had begun to be dominated by those of maintaining and developing spiritual energies. In fact, making the widest allowance for the phenomena of moral retrogression and licence, it would appear that the present 'freedom' of morals has its true cause in the search for a form of union which will be richer and more spiritualizing than that which is limited to the cradle. Here we have a symptom, which may be interpreted as follows.

Within the human mass there floats a certain power of development, represented by the forces of love, which infinitely surpasses the power absorbed in the necessary concern for the reproduction of the species. The old doctrine of chastity assumed that this drive could and should be diverted directly towards God, with no need of support from the creature. In this there was a failure to see that such an energy, still largely potential (as are all the other spiritual powers of matter), also required a long period of development in its natural plane. In the present state of the world, man has not yet, in reality, been completely revealed to himself by woman, nor is the reciprocal revelation complete. In view, therefore, of the evolutive structure of the universe, it is impossible for one to be separated from the other while their development is still continuing. It is not in isolation (whether married or unmarried), but in paired units, that the two portions, masculine and feminine, of nature are to rise up towards God. The view has been put forward that there can be no sexes in spirit. This arises from not having understood that their duality was to be found again in the composition of divinized being. After all, however 'sublimated' man may be imagined to be, he certainly is not a eunuch. Spirituality does not come down upon a 'monad' but upon the human 'dyad'.

There is a general question of the feminine, and so far it has been left unsolved or imperfectly expressed by the Christian theory of sanctity. It is this that accounts for our dissatisfaction with, and our repugnance to, the old discipline of virtue. It used to be urged that the natural manifestations of love should be reduced as much as possible. We now see that the real problem is how to harness the energy they represent and transform them. We must not cut down on them, but go beyond them. Such will be our new ideal of chastity.

III. THE SPIRIT OF CHASTITY

Once we have properly understood and, most important of all, have known by experience, the meaning of the words 'spiritual power of matter', the first thing we see is the disappearance, in an initial phase, of the classic distinction between holiness of body and holiness of spirit. Material creation no longer stretches between man and God like a fog or a barrier. It develops like an elevating, enriching ambience; and it is important not to try to escape from this or release oneself from it, but to accept its reality and make our way through it. Rightly speaking, there are no sacred or profane things, no pure or impure: there is only *a good direction and a bad direction* – the direction of ascent, of amplifying unity, of greatest spiritual effort; and the direction of descent, of constricting egoism, of materializing enjoyment. If they are followed in the direction which leads upwards, all creatures are luminous; if grasped in the direction which leads downwards, they lose their radiance and become, we might almost say, diabolical. According to the skill with which we set our sails to their breeze, it will either capsize our vessel or send it leaping ahead. Hitherto, asceticism has been a pressure towards rejection – the chief requirement of holiness used to be self-deprivation. In future, because of our new moral outlook on matter, spiritual detachment will be something much more like a conquest; it will mean plunging into the flood of created energies, in order both to be uplifted and to uplift them – and *this includes* the first and most fiery of those energies. Chastity (just as resignation, 'poverty', and the other evangelical virtues) is essentially *a spirit*. And so we can begin to see the outline of a general solution to the problem of the feminine.

In itself, *detachment by passing through* is in perfect harmony with the idea of the Incarnation in which Christianity is summed up. The movement carried out by the man who plunges into the world, in order first to share in things and then to carry them along with him – this movement, let me emphasize, is an exact replica of the baptismal act: 'He who descended', says St Paul, 'is he also who ascended . . . that he might fill all things.' It is quite natural, accordingly, that, under the pressure of the sense of man for which she serves as a channel, the Church of God should correct anything rather too 'oriental' (or negative) that might be found in her theory of renunciation. This comparatively new proposition, that Christian perfection consists not so much in purifying oneself from the refuse of the earth as in divinizing creation, is a forward step. In the most conservative quarters, it is beginning to be recognized that there is a communion with God through earth – a sacrament of the world – spreading like a halo round the Eucharist; but there is still a grudging reserve in allotting the share that has at last been accorded to terrestrial sources of nourishment. As in the biblical Eden, the majority of fruits are now allowed to the initiate. His, if he feels their attraction, the 'vocation' – his the joys of artistic creation, the conquests of thought, the emotional excitement of discovery. These broadenings of personality are accepted as sanctifying or patient of sanctification. One tree, however, still carries the initial prohibition, the tree of the feminine. And so we are still faced by the same dilemma – either we can have woman only in marriage, or we must run away from the feminine.

Why this exception? why this departure from logic?

I can distinguish two main reasons: one, a matter of practical prudence – the other, derived from an ideal or theory.

In practice, the feminine is included among natural products that are forbidden as being too dangerous: a disturbing scent, an intoxicating draught. Since the beginning of time, men have been astounded by the uncontrollable power of this element; and in the end, being unable to suppress its use entirely, our mentors have come to limit it to essential cases. There is no distrust (though logically there might well be, perhaps) of the passions for ideas or for numbers, or even of a keen interest in stars or nature. Because these realities are assumed (quite wrongly) to appeal only to the reason, they are regarded as harmless and easily spiritualized. Sexual attraction, on the contrary, is frightening because of the complex and obscure forces it may at any moment bring into operation. Love, it would seem, is a monster slumbering in the depths of our being, and, throughout our lives, we can be safe from it only if we are careful not to disturb its sleep.

I am far from denying the destructive and disintegrating forces of passion. I will go so far as to agree that apart from the reproductive function, men have hitherto used love, on the whole, as an instrument of self-corruption and intoxication. But what do these excesses prove? Because fire consumes and electricity can kill, are we to stop using them? The feminine is the most formidable of the forces of matter. True enough. 'Very well, then,' say the moralists, 'we must keep out of its way.' 'Not at all,' I reply, 'we must master it.' In every domain of the real (physical, affective, intellectual) *'danger' is a sign of*

74

power. Only a mountain can create a terrifying drop. The customary education of the Christian conscience tends to make us confuse tutiorism with prudence, safety with truth. Avoiding the risk of a transgression has become more important to us than carrying a difficult position for God. And it is this that is killing us. 'The more dangerous a thing, the more is its conquest ordained by life': it is from that conviction that the modern world has emerged; and from that our religion, too, must be re-born. In order to justify the overall prohibition that a certain Christian asceticism imposes on the use of the feminine, it is useless to paint a picture of the dangers of an adventure; if we have any 'sporting' instinct, those dangers will only attract us. If we are to abandon our attempt to climb the peak, we need an explanation of why the ascent will not bring us closer to God.

The second reason – a positive reason this time – for excluding the influence of the feminine from the hearts of the fully Christian, is sought by traditional asceticism in the ideal of 'fidelity' which was mentioned at the beginning of this essay. What God asks for from the Christian is his heart; and it is this heart which we have to preserve for him, *without sharing*. But what do we mean by sharing our heart? Is it loving *some thing* outside the lover? Perhaps. But this accepted attachment to the other, whether material or abstract, can be corrected and put right. It is never more than peripheral. What is really serious, and even mortal, is turning towards *an* other: it is loving *some one*. To have a passionate enthusiasm, as a Christian, for science or thought, or any other impersonal structure, is still possible, for its charms are inanimate and can therefore be divinized by us. Woman, however, represents *something personalized*, in other words a type of being that is closed in on itself and is in some way absolute. It is impossible to allow this type into our interior system without to some extent disturbing the unity of attraction which is to elevate us. In the case of love, more than in any other, it is impossible to serve two masters. Such is the final argument of those who defend the 'old' chastity.

In a general way, I must confess that I am suspicious of a doctrine which compares our heart to a glass of water which is emptied when shared. I have already said that I am convinced that our passional power is a delicate organism whose reserves we too often waste when we love ill. But that our heart necessarily becomes less for one being, by giving itself to another (in another relationship or following an hierarchical order), that is something which I find it very difficult to accept. I can find two lovely flowers – and my eyes can return from one with increased sensitivity to the appreciation of the other. Use multiplies power. What is true is that, in the particular case of love, the husband must keep and strengthen for the wife the privileged position which makes her in some way the sun of his interior universe. And it is here that jealousy is in the right: there can be only one sun in our heart's firmament: but why may there not be subordinate stars?

These remarks seem to me already to weaken considerably the psychological value of the 'law of reservation' of the heart, which is invoked by defenders of a chastity 'of privation'. But we can go still further when we answer them. In defining the code of chastity, we have a way of comparing God and the Christian soul to two lovers, *univoce*. This is to overlook the essential fact that God is not a person *of the same order* as ourselves. He is a super-person, a 'hyper-centre' – that is to say someone of greater depth than us. This means that the fact that a man centres his heart on a woman does not *necessarily* imply that that man is going to be affectively 'neutralized' in relation to God. The divine sun (*because* it is deeper) can still be seen *through* the feminine star. It can shine, and with even greater brilliance, along, and reaching beyond, the same line. Even though affectively replete in relation to other human persons, the pair of lovers can still be open, free, and even exalted by their duality, to the higher attraction of God. There is a way of loving which does not merit the apostle's reproach that it 'divides' a man.[7] A purely imaginary case, you will say. Yet are we not, once again, mortally infected by the prevailing confusion between prudential rules and judgements of value? There is no doubt about it: the feminine must be included among the sources from which Christian life draws its vigour. It is exceptional in only one way – in its extreme power. And, precisely because of that power, it, more than any other energy contained in matter, is subject to the triumphant domination of spirit.

Chastity, then, is a virtue of participation and conquest, and not a schooling in restriction and avoidance. Purity is often pictured to us as a fragile crystal which will tarnish or be shattered if it is not protected from rough handling and the light. In fact, it is more like the flame which assimilates everything and brings it up to the standard of its own incandescence. '*Omnia munda mundis*', 'To the pure all things are pure': broadly speaking, that is perfectly true. In the relationship

[7]Chastity attracts, and legitimately, by the aura of *freedom* which surrounds it. There are, it is true, tasks that call for the whole man; but on reflection it becomes apparent that the hindering or dividing agent is not Woman, but either the family or the physically loved woman. A noble passion lends wings. That is why the best test for determining to what degree a love is sublime would be to note to what degree it develops in the direction of a greater freedom of spirit. The more spiritual an affection is, the less it monopolizes – and the more it acts as a spur to action.

between spirit and body everything is, indeed, a matter of
'potential'. 'Burn or be burned.'[8] Volatilize matter or be cor-
rupted by it. Throughout the whole range of things, such is
the law of life: a law which we cannot conceivably avoid if
we are to develop the most sublime peak of our being.

Naturally enough, a price has to be paid for this achievement. In our approaches to woman, and when we come into
contact with her, we are enveloped in a sort of indistinct glow
of illumination – the instinctive feeling that a new world
awaits us and is about to develop in the depths of matter –
if only we fold the wings of spirit, and surrender ourselves to it.
This, in an emotional form (which is much more insidious
than the intellectual form), is the 'materialist illusion'. So: if
we wish to make the mystery of the flesh fully our own, we
must make a considered choice which will be an expression in
our own consciousness of the very effort of creation, and so
discredit the false evidence of the mirage which tends to drag
us down. The truth is, indeed, that love is the threshold of
another universe. Beyond the vibrations with which we are
familiar, the rainbow-like range of its colours is still in full
growth. But, for all the fascination that the lower shades have
for us, it is only towards the 'ultra' that the creation of light
advances. It is in these invisible and, we might almost say,
immaterial zones that we can look for true initiation into
unity. *The depths we attribute to matter are no more than the
reflection of the peaks of spirit.*

[8]Fundamentally, there is a confrontation between two opposing theories of chastity –
two ideas of purity. One side says, 'Above all, break no rule – even at the cost of some
loss in richness.' The other side says, 'Above all, increase your richness, even at the
cost of some contamination.' I need hardly say that, to my mind, it is the latter who
have hold of the truth and will be vindicated by the future.

Both human experience and human thought would appear to guarantee this.

The whole problem now (in theory a secondary problem, but an extremely important one in practice) is to estimate to what degree, as the 'spectrum' turns towards colours of an ever higher quality, the lower radiations continue to shine – or whether they are extinguished. The centre of loving attraction and possession shifts progressively towards the spiritual; and if beings are to attain one another, they are obliged to seek one another at a progressively higher level. But, if they are to ensure the fullness of this sublimation – if they are not to cut the channels which convey to them the spiritual powers of matter – *from what initial level* are they to start taking possession of one another? How much of the body is needed for an optimum of spirit?[9]

And so our analysis of the creative function of chastity-spirit brings us back to the problem of determining the precise meaning and value of virginity.

IV. THE VALUE OF VIRGINITY

As we were saying earlier, the material side of virginity, though important for primitive peoples, has completely ceased to have any significance for us. This, the physical, aspect of the virtue has become meaningless to us. But we have reached the point where we must now consider whether virginity has not some hidden spiritual value, deeper than physical integrity, for the sake of which we may still have reason – better reason, even, than ever – to foster and respect it.

[9]This completes the author's statement of the problem. He now goes on to show the increasing importance of virginity. (Ed.)

On first consideration, the idea of a sanctity that attaches particularly to continence does not seem specially appropriate to the moral significance we have just attributed to chastity. If chastity is a spirit which requires nourishment, why cut it off from the most vigorous of its sources? Is not the gift of the body the complete and natural form in which the natural power of matter offers itself for sublimation? And is not spirit waiting to be produced, like a spark, from the shock of this encounter? And the great surges of energy released by physical love – is it not precisely these which it should be our *first concern* to stimulate, to master, and to transform?

Here I must admit that, left to my own judgement, I am not at all clear about '*quod non licet*', about what is not allowable. For obvious reasons, physical union has traditionally been associated exclusively with the idea of material generation. A certain type of 'theological biology' still teaches indeed that by reason of the human physical conformation it is impossible for it to be otherwise without violating the natural order. As though 'the natural order' of the world were something with which we were presented complete and ready-made, rather than a balance which is trying to establish itself! As though our organs had existed fully formed from the very beginning, and had not, on the contrary, been adapted in the course of evolution to meet new requirements! As though the tongue had *been made* for speech and not *used* for speaking! All that sort of talk rests on very shaky foundations.

The more, accordingly, I think about this problem, the less can I find anything unacceptable in the idea expressed by the heroine of a Russian novel that 'we shall in the end find another way of loving'. Spiritual fecundity accompanying material fecundity ever more closely – and ultimately becoming the *sole* justification of union. Union for the sake of the child – but why not union for the sake of the work, for the sake of the idea? The multiplicity of man is such that each form of association would have its adherents, nor would there be any danger that the second might prematurely destroy the first. Fundamentally, is not this spiritual use of the flesh precisely what many men of genius, men who have been true creators, have instinctively found and adopted, without asking the moralists for their approval? And is it not from these allegedly impure sources that a life has been drawn which here and now sustains those of us to whom conservation is of prime importance?

Looking at the problem abstractly, such is the position I cannot but anticipate. And at the same time, were I to have to leave the field of theory and attempt, or even advise, this practice of spiritual-physical love, I feel that I would be stopped by an insurmountable obstacle – by some indefinable instinct in which I believe I can distinguish something more than the mechanical bent imposed on my soul by continual subjection to the prohibition 'Thou shalt not' repeated for generation after generation. And then I wonder whether it would be a release or only a retrograde step to snap the links of moral duty and reverent admiration that have formed around the ideal of virginity in the course of centuries of human experience. May there not be some hidden reason which ensures that, however omnipotent spirit may be in the domain of chastity, some physical sources of vigour shall not be subject to its transforming power – *precisely because of the perfection of chastity*?

Moralists (as we noted earlier) often seem to us to use an argument based on personal or collective safety to justify exclusion of the flesh from affective relationships – or at any

rate a tendency to reduce its active part to a minimum. It is
something we must deny ourselves, for fear lest we abuse it;
that we must cut ourselves off from, so that we may not be
absorbed by it. We must force ourselves over to the right, to
make sure that we do not slip to the left; climb, to make sure
that we do not fall. By themselves, let me repeat, these reasons
are not sufficient. In the first place it is doubtful whether the
method proposed would be effective. To force often means to
distort; and you can even break a thing by forcing it. No force,
and no idea, has ever been conquered by repression – to do so
you have to harness it. And secondly, if there is one point on
which all religions are in agreement, and on which Christianity
in particular has staked its authority, it is that physical chastity
brings with it a sort of absolute superiority. If, therefore, we
wish to preserve the essence of traditional practice, it is indispensable to disclose some perfection that resides in virginity
by nature.

And it is, I believe, somewhat along the lines that follow
that this may be done. The most penetrating interpretation we
can give of the world – the interpretation we find in much the
same terms in all mystical and philosophical systems – is to
regard the world as a movement of *universal convergence*,
within which the plurality of matter is consummated in spirit.
This view of things takes into account the fundamental and
creative role of erotic attraction. It provides a simple formula
that readily disentangles the complex difficulties presented by
the biological, intellectual and moral evolution of the world. In
every field, it is obvious, progress means unification. Looked
at from this angle, God is seen to be the supreme centre in
which the multiplicity of lower forms of being becomes an

organic whole – the focus at which matter is consummated in spirit. Let us, then, *accept this hypothesis* – and apply it to the problem with which we are now concerned.

At the point at which life, in the present world, has arrived, the spiritualizing unification of human monads is governed by two attractive forces, which are the same in nature but differ in value. These are the mutual love of man and woman, and divine love. As each element seeks to find fulfilment in unity, it is courted simultaneously by the forces of passion and by mystical forces, working *in association*. The element must, *simultaneously*, complete its human unity in the feminine, and its cosmic unity in God. In both, there is fundamentally the same energy of convergence, the same love. The two forces do not, however, pull together in harmony immediately. How, then, are we to combine them and so obtain a resultant force which will give the maximum spiritual 'yield'? That, in fact, is the problem raised by chastity.

A first solution that comes to mind is the very one we suggested at the beginning of this chapter. Initially, man will gravitate to woman. He will take possession of her in the fullest sense; and it is the flame which explodes from this first union which will leap up towards God. First, there is the contact of the two elements in human love; and then the dual ascent towards the greater divine centre. This process, we were saying, seems to have the advantage of most fully releasing, for God, the spiritual potentialities of passion. Without any doubt, it has been responsible for the appearance on earth of great truths and great beauties: but are there reasons why we should be wary of it?

I can see only one – but it is one that could have great weight. It is this: we have just assumed that man's potentialities are magnificently released by physical love. What would appear to have been always dormant in our souls is awakened and leaps forward. Is this completely true? Another possibility suggests itself; that a sort of 'short-circuit' is produced in the dazzling gift of the body – a flash which burns up and deadens a portion of the soul. Something is born, but it is for the most part used up on the spot. What constitutes the peculiar intoxication that comes with complete giving may very well be that in it we burn away a part of our 'absolute'. And so a second solution to the problem of chastity comes to mind. Why should there be this distinction of two phases in union: first one gift, and then another? Is it really possible, without loss, to give oneself twice? The time has perhaps come when, in conformity with the inflexible laws of evolution, man and woman – on whom life has laid the charge of advancing to the highest possible degree the spiritualization of the earth – will have to abandon that way of possessing one another which has hitherto been the only rule for living beings. Retaining of their mutual attraction only that part of it which causes them to rise as they come closer, why should they not direct *forwards* the impulse in which they grasp one another? No immediate contact, but convergence at a higher level: *the moment of complete giving would then coincide with their meeting with the divine.* This retains our faith in the spiritual value of the flesh – but at the same time it finds room for virginity. Chastity becomes in essence a delayed gift.

So we have two solutions, and two roads. Which is right? The evidence that individuals can give on this point is conflicting and contradictory. Congenitally, if I may put it so, I am myself committed to the second. I have followed it as far as possible; and I have, it is true, been through some difficult passages. But I have never felt any impoverishment of being, nor that I had lost my way.

And now I have reached the point where I believe I can distinguish, as I look around me, the two following phases in the creative transformation of human love. During a first phase of humanity, man and woman are confined to the physical act of giving and the concern with reproduction; and around that fundamental act they gradually develop a growing nimbus of spiritual exchanges. At first it was no more than an imperceptible fringe, but the fruitfulness and mystery of union gradually find their way into it; and it is on the side of that nimbus that the balance ultimately comes to rest. However, at that very moment, the centre of physical union from which the light emanated is seen to be incapable of accepting further expansion. The centre of attraction suddenly withdraws ahead, to infinity, we might say; and, in order to continue to possess one another more fully in spirit, the lovers are obliged to turn away from the body, and so seek one another in God. Virginity rests upon chastity as thought upon life: through a reversal of direction, or at one particular point of coincidence.

Such a transformation on the face of the earth cannot, of course, be instantaneous. Time is essentially necessary. When you heat water, the whole quantity does not turn into steam at the same moment: the liquid phase and the gaseous phase exist together for a long time. Nor could it be otherwise. Nevertheless, one single event is taking place beneath this duality – and its significance and 'worth-whileness' extend to the whole. So, at this present moment, physical union retains its necessity and its importance for the race; but its spiritual quality is henceforth defined by the type of higher union it first makes possible and then sustains. Love is going through a 'change of state' in the noosphere; and, if what all the great religions teach us is correct, it is in this new direction that man's collective passage to God is being mapped out.

It is in this form that I picture to myself the evolution of chastity.

Theoretically, this transformation of love is quite possible. All that is needed to effect it is that the pull of the *personal* divine centre be felt with sufficient force to dominate the natural attraction that would tend to cause the pairs of human monads to rush prematurely into one another's arms.

In practice, I am forced to admit, the difficulty of this enterprise seems so great that ninety per cent of my readers would say that all I have written here is over-ingenuous or even wildly absurd. Surely universal experience has shown conclusively that spiritual loves have always ended in grossness? Man is made to walk with his feet on the ground. Has anyone ever thought of giving him wings?

Yes, I shall answer: some madmen have had such a dream; and that is why we have today conquered the skies. What paralyses life is lack of faith and lack of audacity. The difficulty lies not in solving problems but in expressing them. And so we cannot avoid this conclusion: it is biologically evident that to gain control of passion and so make it serve spirit must be a condition of progress. Sooner or later, then, the world will brush aside our incredulity and take this step: because whatever is the more true comes out into the open, and whatever is better is ultimately realized.

The day will come when, after harnessing the ether,[10] the

[10]Writing today, Teilhard would say 'space'. (Ed.)

winds, the tides, gravitation, we shall harness for God the energies of love. And, on that day, for the second time in the history of the world, man will have discovered fire.[11]

Peking, February 1934

[11]As early as 1917, in the very middle of the first world war, Père Teilhard felt himself called to give living expression to this ultimate form of love in God: 'The true union that you ought to seek with creatures that attract you is to be found not by going directly to them, but by converging with them on God, sought in and through them. It is not by making themselves more material, relying solely on physical contacts, but by making themselves more spiritual in the embrace of God, that things draw closer to one another ...' 'The true union is the union that simplifies ... the true fertility is the fertility that brings beings together in the engendering of spirit ...' (*Writings in Time of War*, pp. 143, 197). (Ed.)

THE FUNCTION OF ART
AS AN EXPRESSION OF
HUMAN ENERGY

I AM no artist: I am a geologist – in other words I am simply a prospector whose field is the past; and I have therefore no right to address this gathering. Nevertheless, I have recently had occasion to concern myself with human energy, its value, its use, and its future; and in so doing I have had to examine the various forms assumed by the activity of the world we live in. And this is what I thought I could more or less distinguish, but what only you, who are artists, can see completely, can express unambiguously, and can make real.

In the first place, so far as I understand art, it is a universal perfection which appears as a luminous fringe around every form in which the vital is realized, as soon as the realization attains the perfection of its expression. There is a supreme art in the fish, the bird, the antelope.

In man, however, art, true art, becomes something more than this. It ceases to be a fringe and becomes an object, something endowed with a special life. It becomes individualized; and it then appears in the world as the form assumed in the world by that particular exuberance of energy, released from matter, which characterizes mankind.

A large proportion of this excess of energy in quest of employment is no doubt absorbed by science and philosophy. Science and philosophy would never have been born, nor would they continue to develop, had not the earth possessed, as a result of technological progress, a constantly increasing store of power available for use. At the same time, they are closely connected with the collective fulfilment of the human organism; and we have no difficulty in seeing them as a legitimate and essential extension of life's progress.

In art, on the other hand, we still find, unimpaired, the freedom and even the imaginative fancy, which is characteristic of an ebullition of energy in its native form. In the shimmer of radiance it casts over human civilization, does it not make us think of the countless tints, prodigal and yet without function, which decorate the calyces of flowers or the wings of butter-flies?

The question then arises for the engineer or biologist, whose primary concern is to measure the spiritual yield of things, 'Is art simply a sort of expenditure and dissipation, an escape of human energy? Its characteristic being, as is sometimes said, that it serves no purpose? Or is the contrary true, that this apparent uselessness hides the secret of its practical efficiency?'

As many others have done before me, I have asked myself this question: and it has seemed to me that, far from being a luxury or a parasitical activity, art fulfilled a threefold neces-sary function in the development of spirit throughout the ages.

In the first place, I maintain, art serves to give the over-plus of life which boils up in us the first elementary degree of consistence through which that drive, initially completely internal, begins to be realized objectively for all of us. A feeling may be vivid, but it still lacks something, or cannot be com-municated to others, unless it is expressed in a significant act, in a dance, a song, a cry. It is art that provides this song or cry for the anxieties, the hopes, and the enthusiasms of man. It gives them a body, and in some way materializes them.

Thereby, too, by the very fact that it gives these impulses a sensible form, art idealizes them and already to some degree it intellectualizes them. The artist, I imagine, would be wrong, and indeed has often gone astray, in trying painfully to introduce a thesis or doctrine into his work. In his case, it is intuition and not reason that should be dominant. But if the work does truly issue from the depths of his being, with the richness of musical harmony, then we need have no fear: it will be refracted in the minds of those upon whom it falls, to form a rainbow of light. More primordial than any idea, beauty will be manifest as the herald and generator of ideas.

Through its power of symbolic expression, art thus gives the spiritual energy that is being produced on earth its first body and its first face. But it fulfils a third function in relation to that energy, one that is the most important of all. It communicates to that energy, and preserves for it, its specifically human characteristic, by personalizing it. Science and thought, it is true, call for an incommunicable originality in those who excel in them; but the thinker's originality, or the scientist's, may well be swallowed up in the universality of the conclusions he expresses. The scientist is comparatively soon swamped in the collective creation to which he devotes himself. The artist, precisely because he lives by his imagination, can ignore and counterbalance this cancelling-out of the human worker by his work. The more the world is rationalized and mechanized, the more it needs 'poets' as the ferment within its personality and its preservative.

In short, art represents the area of furthest advance around man's growing energy, the area in which nascent truths condense, take on their first form, and become animate, before they are definitively formulated and assimilated.

This is the effective function and role of art in the general economy of evolution.

Père Teilhard de Chardin's contribution, 13 March 1939, at an artists' luncheon arranged in Paris by the 'Centre d'Etudes des Problèmes humains'.

THE AWAITED WORD

TODAY, in the middle of the global crisis through which the world is passing, there is not a single man, believer or unbeliever, who is not longing with his whole soul for light – a light to show him that there is some sense of direction behind, some outcome to, the confusion that prevails on earth. Never, perhaps, since the first year of the Christian era, has mankind found itself so cut off from its past structures, more anxious about its future – more ready to welcome a saviour.

We who are Christians know that the saviour has already been born; but we now have a completely new phase of mankind, and should not the saviour be *re-born* in a form commensurate with our present needs? People are looking today (this I know from so often having heard it admitted) to Rome. Will the Church be able, at the decisive hour, to take to herself a world which offers itself to her in the very throes of its transformation? Will she find at the critical moment the word which will explain what is happening, and so give back to us clarity of vision and joy in action – the word for which we are waiting?

I myself, a mere unit in the great Christian body, can, you may be sure, make no claim to show our leaders the road to follow. For various accidental reasons, however, and by temperament, I have found myself living more closely than others to the heart of the earth; and in consequence I feel the need to emphasize here, with all sincerity and frankness, the remodelled form of worship I believe to be required by that heart.

I. A POSSIBLE DIAGNOSIS OF THE SITUATION:
A CRISIS OF GROWTH

Some are so distressed by the intellectual and moral disorders that are today confusing the human mass that they are inclined to believe that what we are doing is simply to drop back and disintegrate. Feeling as they do, what they would suggest to save our threatened civilization would be to force emancipated minds back into the framework of the old way of looking at things.

To my mind, the nature of the disease is completely different – and in consequence calls for a completely different remedy. The more I question myself, and the people I meet, the more convinced I am of this: disregard of traditional rules certainly plays a large part in the troubles from which we are suffering, but that disregard itself is not so much lack of principle as dissatisfaction. There is something too narrow and something missing in the gospel as presented to us. In spite of appearances, our age is more religious than ever: it is only that it needs stronger meat. A crisis not of spiritual weakness and frigidity, but one of transformation and growth – that is the sort of ordeal we are experiencing.

That being so, it is useless or even dangerous to recommend a mere return to the past. It is because man needs and hopes for something other that he is now rising up in protest and kicking over the traces. Wider horizons, and not a tighter rein – that, if I am not mistaken, is the only remedy that can effectively bring our generation back to the ways of truth.

But – and this is the point – where are those horizons to be found? Fundamentally, what is it that human beings are

looking for today? In other words, what lies at the root of
their confusion?

II. THE DEEP ROOTS OF THE CRISIS: THE
RISE OF A NEW SUN

At the original source of the intellectual and social troubles
which characterize the present crisis, there lies, to my mind,
an important change; during the last two centuries this change
has taken place surreptitiously in the deepest layers of that
religious consciousness of man which has, with reason, been
called the 'naturally Christian soul'.

Until the dawn of modern times, the problem of salvation
could be expressed for man in no more than two terms: the
existence on earth of each man, and his ultimate end; the brief
years of life, and eternity; the human individual, and God.
And between the two – nothing.

What, then, has happened in the course of barely two
hundred years? As a result of a complex combination of
external discoveries and internal insights, man has become
conscious simultaneously both of the incredible resources
accumulated in the human mass, *and* of the possibilities open
to this energy for the building up of a tangible work, *anticipated*
by nature. God is no longer seen as standing immediately
above man: there is an intermediate magnitude, with its
accompanying train of promises and duties. Thus, without
leaving the world, man is now discovering above himself some
sort of 'object of worship', something greater than himself: and
it is the appearance of the earth of tomorrow – of this new
star, which is channelling into itself the religious forces of the
world – that is associated, I believe, with the origin of our

present perplexities. It is this, in any case, that accounts for the irresistible emergence of the great myths (the communist, the nationalist myths), whose appearance and whose impact are shaking the old civilization. It is no longer a matter of mere heresies within Christianity, but of Christianity's being confronted by what seems to be an entirely new religion, which threatens to make a clean sweep of everything. You may call it the Temptation on the Mountain, if you wish; but there is an infinite subtlety in it, since, in this context, it is not a question of self-gratification in worship, but of disinterested conquest, productive, without any doubt, of lofty spiritual forces. It is the replacement, in human consciousness, of charity by the 'sense of the earth'.

What is the duty of us Christians at this juncture?

III. GENERAL SOLUTION OF THE PROBLEM: CONJUNCTION OF THE TWO STARS IN MANKIND'S HEAVEN

It is impossible, I was saying, to return man to the right path by forcing him back towards some long out-dated condition. And it would be equally useless to try to convert him by removing from his horizon the pseudo-divine object which has just invaded it under the symbols of mankind, of race, or of progress. Whether we like it or not, not one of us can exist without thereby experiencing the deeply penetrating influence of this new star. Each one of us (those of us whose faith is strongest) is faced by the spiritual problem of balancing not two but *three* co-existing realities: our own soul, God, *and also* the earthly future of the world lying ahead of us. To deny the existence of this last object would be to falsify ourselves, to lie to ourselves and, in consequence, to our faith.

If that, however, is so, then the general solution of the problem becomes clear. It emerges automatically. There is only one way of escaping from the threatening, absorbing, thing which we cannot remove from our sky, and must not try to remove, simply because it *exists*: and that way is to overcome it by a Force greater than it. Would it not be possible to assimilate it, to baptize it, to Christianize it, to *Christify* it?

'Thy kingdom come.' We used, perhaps, to imagine that God's triumph is confined to a purely interior and 'supernatural' dominion over souls. Is that true? Or does it not, on the contrary, presuppose not only the tangible reality of our own individual bodies, but also the fulfilment of the collective human organism throughout the ages?

'Love one another.' Is that essentially Christian disposition limited to easing, individually, the sufferings of our fellowmen? Or does it not, rather, need to be developed in active sympathy with the great human body, in such a way as not merely to bind up its wounds but to embrace its anxieties, its hopes, all the structural growth that creation still looks for in it?

To incorporate the progress of the world in our picture of the kingdom of God: to incorporate the sense of the earth, the sense of man, in charity – with the world no longer eclipsing God nor carrying us away at a tangent – with the two stars entering into an harmonious conjunction – with the two influences added together in an hierarchical whole, so to uplift us in one and the same direction – '*Deus amictus mundo*', 'God clothed in the world': were such an operation possible, we may be sure that it would immediately and radically put an end to the internal conflict from which we are suffering.

And so little is needed, so little would be enough, for this liberating transformation to be effected: simply – and this is the point I want to make – that we should follow our creed to its fullest implications, along the logical and historical line of its development.

IV. THE GREAT REMEDY: THE MANIFESTATION OF THE 'UNIVERSAL CHRIST'

'*Nova et vetera*' – 'New things and old.' It is part of the normal economy of the Christian life that certain elements, long dormant in revealed truth, suddenly develop into powerful branches; and this happens commensurately with new times and needs, and in answer to their demands.

In our own day, this, it seems to me, is the part reserved for the grand and essentially dogmatic idea of the Christian *pleroma*: the mysterious synthesis of the uncreated and the created – the grand completion (at once quantitative and qualitative) of the universe in God. It is impossible to read St Paul without being astounded by three things simultaneously: first, the fundamental importance attached by the apostle to this idea, interpreted with the utmost realism; secondly, the relative obscurity to which it has hitherto been relegated by preachers and theologians; and thirdly, its astonishing appropriateness to the religious needs of the present day. Here we have the concept of God gathering to himself not merely a diffuse multiplicity of souls, but the solid, organic, reality of a universe, taken from top to bottom in the complete extent and unity of its energies – and do we not find in that precisely what we were feeling our way towards?

It would, indeed, seem that under the guidance of a divine instinct, and parallel with the rise of modern humanist aspirations, the sap of Christianity is even now flowing into the bud that has been dormant so long, and will soon make it burst into flower. We can now clearly distinguish a fundamental movement in the Church, which also started just two hundred years ago, in the cult based on devotion to the heart of Jesus, and which is now clearly directed towards worship of Christ – of Christ considered in the ways in which he influences the whole mystical body, and in consequence, the whole human social organism; the love of Christ being seen as the energy in which all the chosen elements of creation are fused together without thereby being confused. Rome has recently made a gesture which marks a decisive stage in the development of dogma, expressing and sanctioning in the figure of Christ the King this irresistible advance of Christian consciousness towards a more universalist and more realist appreciation of the Incarnation.

What I have in mind, and what I dream about, is that the Church should follow up the logical extension of this movement, and so make plain and actual to the world, as St Paul did to his converts, the great figure of him in whom the pleroma finds its physical principle, its expression, and its consistence: Christ-Omega, the Universal-Christ. 'Descendit, ascendit, *ut repleret omnia*' – 'He descended, and he ascended, that he might fill all things.'[1] St Paul's imagery made rather a vague impression, no doubt, on the Romans, the Corinthians, the Ephesians, or the Colossians, because in those days the 'world', the 'whole' (with all that those words now imply for us of the organically defined), had not yet come to exist in man's consciousness; but for us, fascinated by the newly discovered magnitude of the universe, it expresses exactly that aspect of

[1] Ephesians 4: 9–10.

God which is needed to satisfy our capacity for worship. Between Christ the King and the Universal Christ, there is perhaps no more than a slight difference of emphasis, but it is nevertheless all-important. It is the whole difference between an external power, which can only be juridical and static, and an internal domination which, inchoate in matter and culminating in grace, operates upon us by and through all the organic linkages of the progressing world.

This figure of the Universal Christ, the prime mover, the saviour, the master and the term of what our age calls evolution, entails no risk, we should note, of the disappearance of the man-Christ, or of a deviation of mysticism into some pantheistic and impersonal form of worship.

The Universal Christ, born from an expansion of the heart of Jesus, requires the historical reality of his human nature if he is not to disappear; and at the same time, as a function of the mechanism specific to love, he does not absorb but completes the personality of the elements which he gathers together at the term of union. Nor, again, is there any danger that the faithful who are drawn to the Universal Christ will forget heaven and allow themselves to succumb to a pagan naturalism and be drawn into a materialist conquest of the earth: for does not the Universal Christ, in his full glory, always emerge from the Cross?

So, there is no danger: on the other hand, what advantages are to be reaped, and how alluring the prospect!

This (and I speak from experience) is something of which I am deeply convinced. The religious consciousness of today, now finally won over to the idea of some 'super-mankind' to be born from our efforts, but unable to find any concrete image or rule of action that will answer its aspirations – this modern consciousness *could never resist* a Christianity which presented itself as the saviour of the earth's most real and living hopes. This would mean a complete and radical conversion of neo-paganism; and it would mean also a new infusion of the lifeblood of mankind into the heart, too often starved of that human energy, of those who believe.

It is only the Christian (and he *only in so far as* he absorbs into himself the humano-divine properties of the Universal Christ) who is in a position today to answer the complex demands of nature and grace by an incredibly rich and simple act, by *a completely synthetic act*, in which the spirit of detachment and the spirit of conquest combine, correct and elevate one another – the spirit of tradition and the spirit of adventurous enquiry, the spirit of the earth and the spirit of God.

May we not say that if the Church wishes to guide the convulsions of the modern world to a fruitful issue, all she needs to do is to summon us to the discovery and the exercise of this completely modern form of charity?

After two thousand years, the affirmation of a Christian optimism in the nativity of the Universal Christ: is not that the message and the rallying cry we need?

Peking, 31 October 1940

Published in 1963 in the Teilhard de Chardin Foundation's *Cahier IV*, without the additions provided later by Fr Bernardino M. Bonansea, O.F.M., of the Catholic University of Washington. These manuscript additions appear in copies given by Père Teilhard to Père Allegra, O.F.M.

A NOTE ON THE
CONCEPT OF CHRISTIAN
PERFECTION

1. IN its time-honoured classic form, the theory of Christian perfection is based on the idea that in the world we know, 'nature' (as opposed to 'super-nature') is fully *complete*. Numerically, of course, spirit is still increasing on earth (i.e. there is a multiplication of souls). Qualitatively, however (in its 'natural' powers), it is at a standstill, making no progress in any direction. All that it is doing is to maintain itself and endure. This being so, human perfection can mean no more than each individual's flight into the supernatural. Anything else is of no concern to the kingdom of God, except in so far as it is necessary to ensure, for some arbitrary period of time, the functioning and preservation of life from age to age: and the children of this world are still on the whole competent to deal with that particular problem. Essentially, the Christian is more purely Christian the more rapidly he detaches himself

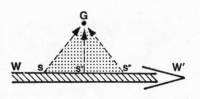

FIGURE I
G = God. s, s′, s″ = souls. WW′ = the world, remaining constant through time. (In this, as in the other figures, 'nature' is represented by cross-hatching, 'the supernatural' by dots.)

from the world; the less he makes use of creatures, the closer he is brought to spirit.

2. But now a new element has just appeared in man's consciousness; and, to my mind, this calls not for a dilution, but for a corrected development, of these traditional views. For many reasons, we are now coming to see that man's powers – both his 'natural powers' and those which are *patient of supernaturalizing'* are *still in full growth* – and that will probably be so for some millions of years to come. We used to think that mankind was fully mature; in fact, it is very far from being adult – very far from being fully created: and this is true not

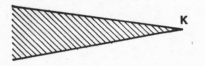

FIGURE 2
The world, converging in the future towards a 'natural', psychic, consummation.

only of its individualized values but also, and most of all, of the *collective term* towards which it is making its way as a result of the great phenomenon of 'convergence of spirit'. We may represent this 'natural' evolution of spirit which creation still awaits by a cone,[1] with apex K (figure 2). How then, are we to conceive the transposition of the problem of perfection into this new context?

3. If we wished to retain the old formulas *literally*, we should obviously have to say that when souls are striving towards holiness they do not have to concern themselves with the

[1] Of course, if anyone rejects this, which is now the normal view for our generation, any further discussion with him becomes useless. We can only wonder how such a man can understand his contemporaries or hope to influence their minds.

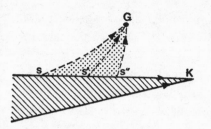

FIGURE 3
The classic formula of
'detachment' applied literally
to a world in process of
natural growth (still active).

formation of the cone K: their perfection consists solely in *detaching* (*separating*) themselves as much as possible from that cone, in the direction of God (figure 3, G). This, however, is no longer possible, for two reasons at least.

a. First, in virtue of the continuing (still active) creation of the 'natural' stuff of the world, the kingdom of God is now seen to be directly concerned, *qua tale*, with a natural process which, after producing the soul of stuff s, must produce that of stuff s', and then that of stuff s" ... The Christian thus finds himself obliged *qua talis*, in as much as he is a Christian, to support the 'natural' world's further progress ahead (since a new form of nourishment, spiritual in substance,[2] is continually to be expected from that progress), and so allow the transforming action of the forces of supernaturalization.

b. But there is a further reason. The serious defect in the solution given by the diagram (figure 3) is that it does not retain the dogmatic magnitude of the Incarnation. In this diagram God, it is true, gathers souls to himself one by one; but he does not consummate in himself the collective development of the world 'as a whole'.[3] He incorporates individuals,

[2]'spiritual in substance' is inserted in the author's hand on the copy given by him to Fr Gabriele M. Allegra, o.f.m., in Peking, between 1942 and 1945. This copy is now in the possession of Fr Allegra's friend, Fr Bernardino M. Bonansea, who has allowed us to use it. (Ed.)

[3]Père Teilhard uses the English phrase. (Ed.)

but the universe and mankind evade him. In consequence, there are *two* distinct spiritual poles in the universe: one natural, K; and the other supernatural, G. In this view of a 'bi-cephalous' spirit, the Incarnation is 'parasitic' to the world: but it does not re-cast the world in a 'mono-cephalous' pleroma, *in Christo*. What would St Paul and the great body of the Greek Fathers have to say to that?

4. The only solution that will satisfy both dogma and reason is that shown diagrammatically in figure 4: that is, the natural and supernatural consummations of the world envelop one another (the latter incorporating and super-animating the former), with God situated on the extended axis of the natural evolution of the whole of spirit. Christogenesis is thus seen to be the sublimation of the whole of cosmogenesis (figure 4).

If the apexes G and K are thus brought together, it is evident that all duality in the mind and heart of the Christian disappears. Without any tendency to deviate into any naturalism or Pelagianism, he finds that he, as much as and *even more than* the unbeliever, can and must have a passionate concern for a terrestrial progress which is essential to the consummation of the kingdom of God. '*Homo sum. Plus et ego.*'

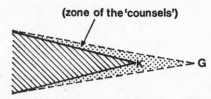

(zone of the 'counsels')

FIGURE 4
This shows diagrammatically the incorporation of natural progress in Christian spiritualization and detachment. K finds completion only in G - and G incorporates K ('needs' K) for the realization of the pleroma.

And at the same time, the elevating power of human detachment is retained *intact*. The Cross still dominates the earth with its symbol of annihilation, but it does so by consecrating and integrating all the sweat and tears – the constructive sweat and tears – which human effort entails. The annihilation is still there, but it is positive annihilation: annihilation, subordinated to a growth, here corresponds to an *excess* of growth – annihilation here requires, if it is to be authentic and possible, that both individuals and the world be ready for, be ripe for, this final step of reversal and excentration. For a fundamental gift of self, one must be *fully self*.

In conclusion, three points should be noted:

a. An important advantage in figure 4 over figure 3, is that it provides our age with a powerful, and perhaps essential, 'credibility motive'. Today, to place God out of tune with human progress is to *undermine* the reasons for belief in the minds of believers, and to *shut the door* of faith in the face of unbelievers (. . . unless we resign ourselves to making the Church into a shelter for the disillusioned).

b. It would be useless and even wrong-headed to look to the saints of the past for explicit approval or condemnation of the new attitude just suggested – since the problem of human progress (as we understand it today) *did not arise* for them. What we need to do, and will in itself be sufficient, is to be able to recognize that when that earlier movement towards perfection is translated into the outlook of today, it becomes precisely the 'detachment by super-attachment' which I have just been describing.[4]

c. At the most fundamental level, what now influences our

---

[4]No longer *separation* (escape) but *emergence* (note added by the author on Fr Allegra's copy).

views on the mechanics (the ascesis) of spiritualization is that spirit has ceased to be for us 'anti-matter', or 'extra-matter', and has become 'trans-matter'. As we now see it, spiritualization can no longer be effected in a breakaway from matter or out of tune with matter: it must be effected by passing through and emerging from matter. '*Descendit, ascendit, ut repleret omnia*', 'He descended, and he ascended, that he might fill all things'[5] – there you have the very economy of the Incarnation.

Peking, 1942

[5] Cf. Ephesians 4: 9–10.

REFLECTIONS ON
HAPPINESS

IN the world of mechanized matter, all bodies obey the laws of a universal gravitation; similarly, in the world of vitalized matter, all organized beings, even the very lowest, steer themselves and progress towards that quarter in which the greatest measure of well-being is to be found.

One might well imagine, then, that a speaker could hardly choose an easier subject than happiness. He is a living being addressing other living beings, and he might well be pardoned for believing that his audience contains none but such as are already in agreement with him and are familiar with his ideas.

In practice, however, the task I have set myself today turns out to be much nicer and more complex.

Like all other animate beings, man, it is true, has an essential craving for happiness. In man, however, this fundamental demand assumes a new and complicated form: for he is not simply a living being with greater sensibility and greater vibratory power than other living beings. By virtue of his 'hominization' he has become a reflective and critical living being; and his gift of reflection brings with it two other formidable properties, the power to perceive what may be possible, and the power to foresee the future. The emergence of this dual power is sufficient to disturb and confuse the hitherto serene and consistent ascent of life. Perception of the possible, and awareness of the future – when these two combine, they not only open up for us an inexhaustible store of hopes and fears, but they also allow those hopes and fears to range far afield in every direction. Where the animal seems to find no difficulties to obstruct its infallible progress towards what will bring it satisfaction, man, on the other hand, cannot take a single step in any direction without meeting a problem for which, ever since he became man, he has constantly and unsuccessfully been trying to find a final and universal solution.

'*De vita beata*', in the ancient phrase – on the happy life: what, in fact, is happiness?

For centuries this has been the subject of endless books, investigations, individual and collective experiments, one after another; and, sad to relate, there has been complete failure to reach unanimity. For many of us, in the end, the only practical conclusion to be drawn from the whole discussion is that it is useless to continue the search. Either the problem is insoluble – there is no true happiness in this world – or there can be only an infinite number of particular solutions – the problem itself defies solution. Being happy is a matter of personal taste. You, for your part, like wine and good living. I prefer cars, poetry, or helping others. 'Liking is as unaccountable as luck.' You must often, I am sure, have heard that sort of remark, and it may well be that you are a little inclined to agree.

What I want to do this evening is to confront fairly and squarely this relativist (and basically pessimist) scepticism shared by so many of our contemporaries, by showing you that, even for man, the general direction in which happiness lies is by no means so ill-defined as it is taken to be: provided always that we confine our enquiry to the search for those joys which are essential and, in so doing, take as our basis what we are taught by science and biology.

I cannot, unfortunately, give you happiness: but I do hope that I may be able at least to help you find it.

What I have to say falls into two parts. In the first, which will be primarily theoretical, we shall try together to define the best route leading to human happiness.

In the second part, which will serve as a conclusion, we shall consider how we must adapt our individual lives to these general axes which run towards happiness.

1. The Theoretical Axes of Happiness

A. THE ROOT OF THE PROBLEM: THREE DIFFERENT ATTITUDES TO LIFE

If we are to understand more clearly how the problem of happiness presents itself to us, and why we find ourselves at a loss when we meet it, it is essential to start by taking a comprehensive view of the whole position. By this I mean that we must distinguish three fundamental initial attitudes to life adopted by men as a matter *of fact*.

Here an analogy may well be a useful guide.

Let us imagine a party of tourists who have set out to climb a difficult peak, and let us take a look at them some hours after they have started. By this time we may suppose the party to be divided into three sorts of elements.

Some are regretting having left the inn. The fatigue and risks involved seem out of all proportion to the value of a successful climb. They decide to turn back.

Others are not sorry that they set out. The sun is shining, and there is a beautiful view. But what is the point of climbing any higher? Surely it is better to enjoy the mountain from here, in the open meadow or deep in the wood. And so they stretch out on the grass, or explore the neighbourhood until it is time for a picnic meal.

And lastly there are the others, the real mountaineers, who keep their eyes fixed on the peaks they have sworn to climb. So they set out again.

The tired – the hedonists – the enthusiasts.

Three types of men: and, deep within our own selves, we hold the germ of all three. And, what is more, it is into these three types that the mankind in which we live and move has always been divided.

1. *First, the tired (or the pessimists)*

For this first category of men, existence is a mistake or a failure. We do not fit in – and so the best thing we can do is, as gracefully as possible, to retire from the game. If this attitude is carried to its extreme, and expressed in terms of a learned doctrinal system, it leads in the end to the wisdom of the Hindus, according to which the universe is an illusion and a prison – or to a pessimism such as Schopenhauer's. But, in a milder and commoner form, the same attitude emerges and can be recognized in any number of practical decisions that are only too familiar to you. 'What is the good of trying to find the answer? ... Why not leave the savages to their savagery and the ignorant to their ignorance? What is the point of science? What is the point of the machine? Is it not better to lie down than to stand up? better to be dead than asleep in bed?' And all this amounts to saying, at least by implication, that it is better to be less than to be more – and that best of all would be not to be at all.

2. *Secondly, the hedonists* (*or pleasure-seekers*)

For men of this second type, to be is certainly better than not to be. But we must be careful to note that in this case 'to be' has a special meaning. For the followers of this school, to be, or to live, does not mean to act, but simply to take your fill of this present moment. To enjoy each moment and each thing, husbanding it jealously so that nothing of it be allowed to be lost – and above all with no thought of shifting one's ground – that is what they mean by wisdom. When we have had enough, then we can lie back on the grass, or stretch our legs, or look at the view from another spot. And meanwhile, what is more, we shall not rule out the possibility of turning back downhill. We refuse, however, to risk anything for the sake of or on the chance of the future – unless, in an over-refinement of sensibility, danger incurred for its own sake goes to our heads, whether it be in order to enjoy the thrill of taking a chance or to feel the shuddering grip of fear.

This is our own version, in an oversimplified form, of the old pagan hedonism found in the school of Epicurus. In literary circles such has recently been the tendency, at any rate, of a Paul Morand or a Montherlant – or (and here it is far more subtle) of a Gide (the Gide of *Fruits of the Earth*), whose ideal of life is to drink without ever quenching (rather, indeed, in such a way as to increase) one's thirst – and this with no idea of restoring one's vigour, but simply from a desire to drain, ever more avidly, each new source.

3. *Finally, the enthusiasts*

By these I mean those for whom living is an ascent and a discovery. To men in this third category, not only is it better to be than not to be, but they are convinced that it is always possible – and the possibility has a unique value – to attain a fuller measure of being. For these conquerors, enamoured of the adventurous, being is inexhaustible – not in Gide's way, like a precious stone with innumerable facets which one can never tire of turning round and round – but like a focus of warmth and light to which one can always draw closer. We may laugh at such men and say that they are ingenuous, or we may find them tiresome; but at the same time it is they who have made us what we are, and it is from them that tomorrow's earth is going to emerge.

Pessimism and return to the past; enjoyment of the present moment; drive towards the future. There, as I was saying, we have three fundamental attitudes to life. Inevitably, therefore, we find ourselves back at the very heart of our subject: a confrontation between three contrasting forms of happiness.

1. *First, the happiness of tranquillity*

No worry, no risk, no effort. Let us cut down our contacts, let us restrict our needs, let us dim our lights, toughen our protective skin, withdraw into our shell. – The happy man is the man who attains a minimum of thought, feeling and desire.

2. Secondly, the happiness of pleasure

Static pleasure or, better still, pleasure that is constantly re-newed. The goal of life is not to act and create, but to make use of opportunities. And this again means less effort, or no more effort than is needed to reach out for a clean glass or a fresh drink. Lie back and relax as much as possible, like a leaf drinking in the rays of the sun – shift your position constantly so that you may feel more fully: that is the recipe for happiness. – The happy man is the man who can savour to the highest degree the moment he holds in his hands.

3. Finally, the happiness of growth

From this third point of view, happiness has no existence nor value in itself as an object which we can pursue and attain as such. It is no more than the sign, the effect, the reward (we might say) of appropriately directed action: a by-product, as Aldous Huxley says somewhere, of effort. Modern hedonism is wrong, accordingly, in suggesting that some sort of renewal of ourselves, no matter what form it takes, is all that is needed for happiness. Something more is required, for no change brings happiness unless the way in which it is effected involves an *ascent*. – The happy man is therefore the man who, without any direct search for happiness, inevitably finds joy as an added bonus in the act of forging ahead and attaining the full-ness and finality of his own self.

Happiness of tranquillity, happiness of pleasure, and happi-ness of development: we have only to look around us to see that at the level of man it is between these three lines of pro-gress that life hesitates and its current is divided.

Is it true, as we are so often told, that our choice is determined only by the dictates of individual taste and temperament?

Or is the contrary true? that somewhere we can find a reason, indisputable because objective, for deciding that one of these three roads is absolutely the best, and is therefore the only road which can lead us to real happiness?

B. THE ANSWER GIVEN BY THE FACTS

1. *General solution: fuller consciousness as the goal*

For my part, I am absolutely convinced that such a criterion, indisputable and objective, does exist – and that it is not mysterious and hidden away but lies open for all to see. I hold, too, that in order to see it all we have to do is to look around and examine nature in the light of the most recent achievements of physics and biology – in the light, that is, of our new ideas about the great phenomenon of evolution.

The time has come, as you must know, when nobody any longer retains any serious doubts about this: the universe is not 'ontologically' fixed – in the very depths of its entire mass it has from the beginning of time been moving in two great opposing currents. One of these carries matter towards states of extreme disintegration; the other leads to the building up of organic units, the higher types of which are of astronomical complexity and form what we call the 'living world'.

That being so, let us consider the second of these two currents, the current of life, to which we belong. For a century or more, scientists, while admitting the reality of a biological evolution, have been debating whether the movement in which we are caught up is no more than a sort of vortex, revolving in a closed circle; or whether it corresponds to a clearly defined drift, which carries the animate portion of the world towards some specific higher state. There is today almost unanimous agreement that it is the second of these hypotheses which would appear undoubtedly to correspond to reality. Life does not develop complexity without laws, simply by chance. Whether we consider it as a whole or in detail, by examining organic beings, it progresses methodically and irreversibly towards ever higher states of consciousness. Thus the final, and quite recent, appearance of man on the earth is only the logical and consistent result of a process whose first stages were already initiated at the very origins of our planet.

Historically, life (which means in fact the universe itself, considered in its most active portion) is a rise of consciousness. How this proposition directly affects our interior attitudes and ways of behaviour must, I suggest, be immediately apparent.

We talk endlessly, as I was saying a moment ago, about what is the best attitude to adopt when we are confronted by our own lives. Yet, when we talk in this way, are we not like a passenger in the Paris to Marseilles express who is still wondering whether he ought to be travelling north or south? We go on debating the point: but to what purpose, since the decision has already been taken without reference to ourselves, and here we are on board the train? For more than four hundred million years, on this earth of ours (or it would be more correct to say, since the beginning of time, in the universe), the vast mass of beings of which we form a part has been tenaciously and tirelessly climbing towards a fuller measure of freedom, of sensibility, of inner vision. And are we still wondering whither we should be bound?

The truth is that the shadow of the false problems vanishes

in the light of the great cosmic laws. Unless we are to be guilty of a physical contradiction (unless, that is, we deny everything that we are and everything that has made us what we are) we are all obliged, each of us on his own account, to accept the primordial choice which is built into the world of which we are the reflective elements. If we withdraw in order to diminish our being, and if we stand still to enjoy what we have, in each case we find that the attempt to run counter to the universal stream is illogical and impossible.

The road to the left, then, and the road to the right are both closed: the only way out is straight ahead.

Scientifically and objectively, only one answer can be made to the demands of life: the advance of progress.

In consequence, and again scientifically and objectively, the only true happiness is the happiness we have described as the happiness of growth and movement.

Do we want to be happy, as the world is happy, and with the world? Then we must let the tired and the pessimists lag behind. We must let the hedonists take their homely ease, lounging on the grassy slope, while we ourselves boldly join the group of those who are ready to dare the climb to the topmost peak. Press on!

Even so, to have chosen the climb is not enough. We have still to make sure of the right path. To get up on our feet ready for the start is well enough. But, if we are to have a successful and enjoyable climb, which is the best route?

2. *Detailed solution: the three phases of personalization*

As I said earlier, life in the world continually rises towards greater consciousness, proportionate to greater complexity –

as though the increasing complexity of organisms had the effect of deepening the centre of their being.

Let us consider, then, how this advance towards the highest unity actually works out in detail; and, for the sake of clarity and simplicity, let us confine ourselves to the case of man – man, who is psychically the highest of all living beings and the one best known to us.

When we examine the process of our inner unification, that is to say of our personalization, we can distinguish three allied and successive stages, or steps, or movements. If man is to be fully himself and fully living, he must, (1) be centred upon himself; (2) be 'de-centred' upon 'the other'; (3) be super-centred upon a being greater than himself.

We must define and explain in turn these three forward movements, with which (since happiness, we have decided, is an effect of growth) three forms of attaining happiness must correspond.

1. First, *centration*. Not only physically, but intellectually and morally too, man is man only if he cultivates himself – and that does not mean simply up to the age of twenty ... If we are to be fully ourselves we must therefore work all our lives at our organic development: by which I mean that we must constantly introduce more order and more unity into our ideas, our feelings and our behaviour. In this lies the whole programme of action, and the whole value and meaning (all the hard work, too!) of our interior life, with its inevitable drive towards things that are ever-increasingly spiritual and elevated. During this first phase each one of us has to take up again and repeat, working on his own account, the general labour of life. Being is in the first place making and finding one's own self.

2. Secondly, *decentration*. An elementary temptation or illusion lies in wait for the reflective centre which each one of us nurses deep inside him. It is present from the very birth of that centre; and it consists in fancying that in order to grow greater each of us should withdraw into the isolation of his own self, and egoistically pursue in himself alone the work, peculiar to him, of his own fulfilment: that we must cut ourselves off from others, or translate everything into terms of ourselves. However, there is not just one single man on the earth. That there are, on the contrary, and necessarily must be, myriads and myriads at the same time is only too obvious. And yet, when we look at that fact in the general context of physics, it takes on a cardinal importance – for it means, quite simply, this: that, however individualized by nature thinking beings may be, each man still represents no more than an atom, or (if you prefer the phrase) a very large molecule; in common with all the other similar molecules, he forms a definite corpuscular system from which he cannot escape. Physically and biologically man, like everything else that exists in nature, is essentially plural. He is correctly described as a 'mass-phenomenon'. This means that, broadly speaking, we cannot reach our own ultimate without emerging from ourselves by uniting ourselves with others, in such a way as to develop through this union an added measure of consciousness – a process which conforms to the great law of complexity. Hence the insistence, the deep surge, of love, which, in all its forms, drives us to associate our individual centre with other chosen and specially favoured centres: love, whose essential function and charm are that it completes us.

3. Finally, *super-centration*. Although this is less obvious, it is ✗ absolutely necessary to understand it.

If we are to be fully ourselves, as I was saying, we find that we are obliged to enlarge the base on which our being rests; in other words, we have to add to ourselves something of 'the Other'. Once a small number of centres of affection have been initiated (some special circumstances determining their choice), this expansive movement knows no check. Imperceptibly, and by degrees, it draws us into circles of ever-increasing radius. This is particularly noticeable in the world of today. From the very beginning, no doubt, man has been conscious of belonging to one single great mankind. It is only, however, for our modern generations that this indistinct social sense is beginning to take on its full and real meaning. Throughout the last ten millennia (which is the period which has brought the sudden speeding-up of civilization) men have surrendered themselves, with but little reflection, to the multiple forces (more profound than any war) which were gradually bringing them into closer contact with one another; but now our eyes are opening, and we are beginning to see two things. The first is that the closed surface of the earth is a constricting and inelastic mould, within which, under the pressure of an ever-increasing population and the tightening of economic links, we human beings are already forming but one single body. And the second thing is that through the gradual building-up within that body of a uniform and universal system of industry and science our thoughts are tending more and more to function like the cells of one and the same brain. This must inevitably mean that as the transformation follows its natural line of progress we can foresee the time when men will understand what it is, animated by one single heart, to be united together in wanting, hoping for, and loving the same things at the same time.

The mankind of tomorrow is emerging from the mists of the future, and we can actually see it taking shape: a 'super-mankind', much more conscious, much more powerful, and much more unanimous than our own. And at the same time (a point to which I shall return) we can detect an underlying but deeply rooted feeling that if we are to reach the ultimate of our own selves, we must do more than link our own being with a handful of other beings selected from the thousands that surround us: we must form one whole with all simultaneously.

We can draw but one conclusion from this twofold phenomenon which operates both outside ourselves and inside ourselves: that what life ultimately calls upon us to do in order that we may be, is to incorporate ourselves into, and to subordinate ourselves to, an organic totality of which, cosmically speaking, we are no more than conscious particles. Awaiting us is a centre of a higher order – and already we can distinguish it – not simply beside us, but *beyond* and *above* us.

We must, then, do more than develop our own selves – more than give ourselves to another who is our equal – we must surrender and attach our lives to one who is greater than ourselves.

In other words: first, be. Secondly, love. Finally, worship.

Such are the natural phases of our personalization.

These, you must understand, are three linked steps in life's upward progress; and they are in consequence three superimposed stages of happiness – if, as we have agreed, happiness is indissolubly associated with the deliberate act of climbing.

The happiness of growing greater – of loving – of worshipping.

Taking as our starting-point the laws of life, this, to put it in a nutshell, is the triple beatitude which is theoretically foreseeable.

Now what is the verdict of experience on this point? Let us for a moment go directly to the facts, and use them to check the accuracy of our deductions.

First, there is the happiness of that deep-seated growth in one's own self – growth in capabilities, in sensibility, in self-possession. Then, too, there is the happiness of union with one another, effected between bodies and souls that are made to complete one another and come together as one.

I have little need to emphasize the purity and intensity of these two first forms of joy. Everybody is in basic agreement on that point.

But what shall we say about the happiness of sinking and losing self in the future, in one greater than ourselves? . . . Is not this pure theorizing or dreaming? To find joy in what is out of scale with us, in what we can as yet neither touch nor see. Apart from a few visionaries, is there anyone in the positivist and materialist world we are forced to live in who can concern himself with such an idea?

Who, indeed?

And yet, consider for a moment what is happening around us.

Some months ago, at a similar meeting, I was telling you about the two Curies – the husband and wife who found happiness in embarking on a venture, the discovery of radium, in which they realized that to lose their life was to gain it. Just think, then: how many other men (in a more modest way, maybe, and in different forms and circumstances), yesterday and today, have been possessed, or are still possessed, even to the point of death, by the demon of research? Try to count them.

In the Arctic and Antarctic: Nansen, Andrée, Shackleton, Charcot, and any number of others.

The men of the great peaks: the climbers of Everest.

The laboratory workers who ran such risks: killed by rays or by the substances they handled – victims of a self-injected disease.

Add to these the legion of aviators who conquered the air. And those, too, who shared man's conquest of man: all who risked, or indeed gave, their lives for an idea.[1]

Make a rough count; and when you have done so, take the writings and letters left by these men (such of them as left any), from the most noteworthy of them (the everyday names) to the most humble (those whose names are not even known) – the airmail pilots who twenty-five years ago were pioneering the air-route across America for human thoughts and loves, and paid for it, one after another, with their lives. What do you find when you read what they confided to paper? You find joy, a joy that is both higher and deeper – a joy full of power: the explosive joy of a life that has at last found a *boundless* area in which to expand.

Joy, I repeat, in that which knows no bounds.

What generally saps and poisons our happiness is that we feel that we shall so soon exhaust and reach the end of whatever it is that attracts us: we know the pain of separation, of loss by attrition – the agony of seeing time fly past, the terror of knowing how fragile are the good things we hold, the dis-

---

[1] 'You know that my life is an oblation, joyfully and conscientiously offered, with no selfish hope of reward, to the Power which is higher than life' (Rathenau).

appointment of coming so soon to the end of what we are and of what we love.

But when a man has found, in an ideal or a cause, the secret of collaboration and self-identification (whether it be close or distant) with the universe as it advances, then all those dark shadows disappear. The joy of worshipping so spreads over the joy of being and the joy of loving as to allow them to expand and grow firmer (Curie, for example, and Termier were admirable friends, fathers and husbands): it does not lessen or destroy the earlier joys, and it holds and brings with it, in its fullness, a wonderful peace. Its source of nourishment is inexhaustible, because it gradually becomes one with the very consummation of the world in which we move; by the same token, moreover, it is safe from every threat of death and decay. Finally, it is, in one way or another, constantly within our reach, since the best way we have of reaching it is simply, each one of us in his own place, to do what we are able to do as well as we can.

The joy of the element which has become conscious of the whole which it serves and in which it finds fulfilment – the joy which the reflective atom draws from awareness of its function and completion within the universe which contains it – this, both logically and factually, is the highest and most progressive form of happiness I can put before you and hope that you may attain.

2. The Fundamental Rules of Happiness

So much for pure theory. We may now consider in what ways it can be applied to our individual lives.

We have just made it clear that true happiness is a happiness of growth – and, as such, it awaits us in a quarter characterized by:

1. unification of self within our own selves;

2. union of our own being with other beings who are our equals;

3. subordination of our own life to a life which is greater than ours.

What consequences do these definitions entail for our day-to-day conduct? And what practical action should we take in order to be happy?

I can, of course, satisfy your curiosity and assist your good will by only the most general indications; for it is here that, quite rightly, we come up against any number of problems of taste, accident and temperament. Life becomes established and progresses in nature and structure only by reason of the very great variety of its elements. Each one of us sees the world and makes his approach to it from a particular angle, backed by a reserve of vital energy, with its own peculiarities, which cannot be shared by others. (We may note, incidentally, that it is this complementary diversity which underlies the biological value of 'personality'.) Each one of us, therefore, is the only person who can ultimately discover for himself the attitude, the approach (which nobody else can imitate), which will make him cohere to the utmost possible degree with the surrounding universe as it continues its progress; that cohesion being, in fact, a state of peace which brings happiness.

Bearing these reservations in mind, we can, following our earlier lines of thought, draw up the following three rules of happiness.

1. If we are to be happy, we must first react against our tendency

to follow the line of least resistance, which causes us either to remain as we are, or to look primarily to activities external to ourselves for what will provide new impetus to our lives. We must, it is true, sink our roots deep into the rich, tangible, material realities which surround us; but in the end it is by working to achieve our own inner perfection – intellectual, artistic, moral – that we shall find happiness. The most important thing in life, Nansen used to say, is to find oneself. Through and beyond matter, spirit is hard at work, building. – *Centration.*

2. If we are to be happy we must, secondly, react against the selfishness which causes us either to close in on ourselves, or to force our domination upon others. There is a way of loving – a bad and sterile way – by which we try to possess rather than to give ourselves. Here again, in the case of the couple or the group, we meet that same law of maximum effort which governed the progress of our interior development. The only love which brings true happiness is that which is expressed in a spiritual progress effected in common. – *Decentration.*

3. And if we are to be happy – completely happy – we must, thirdly, in one way or another, directly or through some medium which gradually reaches out further afield (a line of research, a venture, an idea, perhaps, or a cause), transfer the ultimate interest of our lives to the advancement and success of the world we live in. If we are to reach the zone where the great permanent sources of joy are to be found, we must be like the Curies, like Termier and Nansen, like the first aviators and all the pioneers I spoke of earlier: we must re-polarize our lives upon one greater than ourselves. Do not be afraid that this

means that if we are to be happy we must perform some remarkable feat or do something quite out of the ordinary; we have only to do what any one of us is capable of: become conscious of our living solidarity with one great Thing, and then do the smallest thing in a great way. We must add one stitch, no matter how small it be, to the magnificent tapestry of life; we must discern the Immense which is building up and whose magnetic pull is exerted at the very heart of our own humblest activities and at their term; we must discern it and cling to it – when all is said and done, that is the great secret of happiness. As one of the most acute, and most materialist, thinkers of modern England, Bertrand Russell, has put it: it is in a deep and instinctive union with the whole current of life that the greatest of all joys is to be found. – *Super-centration.*

There you have the real core of what I have to say to you; but, having reached that point, there is one more thing which I owe it to you and to myself to say, if I am to be absolutely truthful.

I was recently reading a curious book,[2] in which the English novelist and thinker H. G. Wells writes about the original views recorded earlier by an American biologist and businessman, William Burrough Steele, which bear precisely on the point we are now considering, human happiness. Steele tries, with much good sense and cogency, to show (just as I have been doing) that since happiness cannot be dissociated from some notion of immortality, man cannot hope to be fully happy unless he sinks his own interests and hopes in those of the world, and more particularly in those of mankind. He adds, however, that, put in those terms, the solution is still incom-

[2]H. G. Wells, *The Anatomy of Frustration.*

plete; for if we are to be able to make a complete gift of self we must be able to love. And how can one love a collective, impersonal reality – a reality that in some respects must seem monstrous – such as the world, or even mankind?

The objection which Steele found when he looked deeper, and to which he gave no answer, is terribly and cruelly to the point. My treatment of the subject would, therefore, be both incomplete and disingenuous if I did not point out to you that the undeniable movement which, as we can see, is leading the mass of mankind to place itself at the service of progress is not 'self-sufficient': If this terrestrial drive which I am asking you to share is to be sustained, it must be harmonized and synthesized with the Christian drive.

We can look around and note how the mysticism of research and the social mysticisms are advancing, with admirable faith, towards the conquest of the future. Yet no clearly defined summit, and, what is more serious, no *lovable* object is there for them to worship. That is the basic reason why the enthusiasm and the devotion they arouse are hard, arid, cold, and sad: to an observer they can only be a cause for anxiety, and to those who aspire to them they can bring only an incomplete happiness.

At the same time, parallel with these human mysticisms, and until now only marginal to them, there is Christian mysticism; and for the last two thousand years this has constantly been developing more profoundly (though few realize this) its view of a personal God: a God who not only creates but animates and gives totality to a universe which he gathers to himself by means of all those forces which we group together under the name of evolution. Under the persistent pressure of Christian thought, the infinitely distressing vastness of the world is

gradually converging upwards, to the point where it is transfigured into a focus of loving energy.

Surely, then, we cannot fail to see that these two powerful
currents between which the force of man's religious energies is
divided – the current of human progress, and the current of
all-embracing charity – need but one thing, to run together,
and complete one another?

Suppose, first, that the youthful surge of human aspirations,
fantastically reinforced by our new concepts of time and space,
of matter and life, should make its way into the life-stream of
Christianity, enriching and invigorating it; and suppose at the
same time, too, that the wholly modern figure of a universal
Christ, such as is even now being developed by Christian
consciousness, should stand, should burst into sight, should
spread its radiance, at the peak of our dreams of progress, and so
give them precision, humanize and personalize them. Would
not this be an answer, or rather *the* complete answer, to the
difficulties before which our action hesitates?

Unless it receives a new blood transfusion from matter,
Christian spirituality may well lose its vigour and become lost
in the clouds. And, even more certainly, unless man's sense of
progress receives an infusion from some principle of universal
love, it may well turn away with horror from the terrifying
cosmic machine in which it finds itself involved.

If we join the head to the body – the base to the peak – then,
suddenly, there comes a surge of plenitude.

To tell you the truth, I see the complete solution to the
problem of happiness in the direction of a Christian humanism:
or, if you prefer the phrase, in the direction of a super-human
Christianity within which every man will one day understand
that, at all times and in all circumstances, it is possible for him

not only to serve (for serving is not enough) but to cherish in all things (the most forbidding and tedious, no less than the loveliest and most attractive) a universe which, in its evolution, is charged with love.[3]

Lecture given by Père Teilhard de Chardin in Peking, 28 December 1943

[3]Père Teilhard had added the following quotation at the end of his original typescript: 'From the religious standpoint happiness and contentment are not things which result from welfare in any mere material or biological sense. Were human society freed from all disease or accident, poverty, and overt crime, it might still be very miserable and intolerably dull. The only thing that brings content is the service of God; and that service can be equally real under the most variable conditions and in any station in life; for the kingdom of God is within us. God's kingdom is one of loyal service, whatever form the service may take. The religious perception that in that service, apart from its mere outward results, we are one with God, brings inspiration, strength, and inward contentment' (J. B. S. Haldane, *Materialism*, Hodder & Stoughton, London, 1932, p. 156).

CAN MORAL SCIENCE
DISPENSE WITH A
METAPHYSICAL FOUNDATION?

THE first thing we have to do is to define 'moral science' and 'metaphysics'.

Moral Science
a. In the widest sense, we may apply the term 'moral science' to every coherent system of action, accepted by necessity or agreement. (In this sense one could speak of the 'moral science' of a game of chess.)
b. In the strict sense, 'moral science' is a coherent system of action which is
 – universal (governing the whole of human activity)
 – and categorical (entailing some form of obligation).

Metaphysics
In what follows, metaphysics is to be taken as meaning every solution or vision of the world (of life) 'as a whole' (every *Weltanschauung*), whether that solution of the complete world imposes itself on our intelligence, or whether it is adhered to categorically as a choice or a postulate.

Once these two definitions are accepted, the question we have asked is immediately answered, simply by confronting each of the two terms with the other. If, in fact, moral science (in the strict sense of the words) implies *coherence* of action with

– either a universal equilibrium (static moral systems)

– or a universal movement (dynamic moral systems)

then it necessarily *presupposes* the categorical acceptance of a certain view of the world (as being in equilibrium or in evolution); otherwise it is 'up in the air' – indeterminate.

It follows, then, that moral science and metaphysics must inevitably be seen as, structurally, the two aspects (the intellectual and the practical) of one and the same system. A metaphysics is necessarily backed by a moral science, and vice versa. Every metaphysics entails its own moral science, and every moral science implies its own metaphysics. Essentially the two go together *in pairs*. There are as many definitions of good and evil, as many forms of obligation, as there are solutions to the world.

From the philosophical primacy accorded to the individual are derived the 'egoist' moral systems.

From the philosophical primacy of society, the social.

From the philosophical primacy of race, the 'national-socialist'.

From the philosophical primacy of enjoyment, the 'hedonistic'.

From the philosophical primacy of knowledge, the heuristic.

From the philosophical primacy of humanity, the humanist.

And finally, to philosophical agnosticism, corresponds a-moralism.

In every case, we should note, *obligation* is a function of the solidarity and inter-dependence which the philosophical system establishes between individual freedom and the universe. The more an individual, as a consequence of his metaphysical convictions, recognizes that he is an *element* of a universe in which he finds his fulfilment, the more closely he feels that he is bound from *within* himself to the duty of conforming to the laws of the universe. In those philosophies in which the universe culminates in a personal and transcendent being, this immanent obligation is *backed* and *reinforced* by a transcendent obligation of loving obedience to the will of God.

In theory, all this seems strictly true. In practice, no doubt, many men act in a moral way *by instinct or by temperament*. Such fidelity, however, is logically *justified* only by implicit acceptance of a certain vision of the world, in other words, a certain metaphysics.

For example, if philanthropical feelings are to be justified, it is essential to have a certain view of the world in which human individuals are seen to be linked together in the unity of a common destiny.

Similarly, if an enthusiasm for enquiry and progress in all its forms is to be justified, there must at all costs be an optimistic and progressive theory of the universe, extending to a demand for some irreversibility in the developments of spirit.[1]

It follows from this organic and fundamental relation between moral science and metaphysics that our intellectual adherence to a particular philosophy is a complex phenomenon, in which the operation of the reason and the will are intricately combined: for if the choice of a moral system follows logically from rational adherence to a metaphysics, on the other hand a metaphysics is ultimately acceptable to us, and appeals to us, only in so far as it enables our active side to be developed as fully as we wish it to be.

---

[1]However 'empirical' it may claim to be, a moral system cannot avoid attributing a certain primacy, be it to well-being, to pleasure, to success . . . and every one of these primacies (and the very definition of the word 'success') implies essentially a solution or vision of the world as a whole – in other words, a metaphysics.

The test of a metaphysics is the moral system which is derived from it.

Today we are feeling the influence of new 'evolutive' views, and these, it would appear, are causing the mass of mankind to turn towards a moral system in which primacy is accorded to hard work and human unity (a system which accepts movement and looks to an ideal). This is linked with a metaphysics in which the universe is seen as a quantum of psychic energy flowing towards higher states of consciousness and spirituality.

There is a final difficulty: is the metaphysics to which every moral system looks for a *backing*, a true structural complement, or merely a fabricated justification, a sort of disease[2] of the mind? And the answer: it is a structural complement, because –

1. This metaphysics provides the necessary animating force.

2. It determines the modes and progressive developments of action.

Peking, 23 April 1945

[2]Père Teilhard uses the English word. (Ed.)

THE SPIRITUAL CONTRIBUTION
OF THE FAR EAST:
SOME PERSONAL REFLECTIONS

THIS is a critical period for mankind. With an intense feeling of its own power and, at the same time, an equally intense feeling of its inner disintegration, it is looking desperately for a soul; and today it is once again towards the East that many are directing their search, wondering if it may not be in that quarter that the first signs of the dawn will be seen. The East stands for spirit, the West for matter. Such, they keep telling us from over there, was the plan on which the world was divided between the children of earth.

I have, myself, no special competence in the history of Asiatic thought; but, simply as a considered reaction to an environment in which I have been deeply involved for a long time, I would like in what follows to offer a few remarks which, I believe, reduce to its correct and substantially valid proportions the spiritual contribution we are justified in expecting from our fellow human beings in the Far East.

I. FORMS OF SPIRITUALITY IN THE FAR EAST

Many Westerners have a vague and distant picture of the Far East as bathed, throughout its whole extent, in a sort of Buddhist serenity. It is a view that has been popularized by tourists' reports, by novels, and by the countless curios brought home by travellers.

In reality, however, there are profound differences underlying this generally accepted uniformity; and we can form a
preliminary idea of these by taking as representative and considering in turn the three great segments into which, broadly
speaking, the east-Asian land mass is divided: India, China, and
Japan.

a. Spiritually speaking, what makes India is an extraordinary,
a predominant, sense of the one and of the divine. By an
astonishing reversal of what happens among us in the West,
for the Hindu the world is in some way less clear than God:
so much so, that it is the world and not God whose existence
presents difficulty to the intelligence and needs to be justified.
The invisible is more real than the visible: that is the fundamental religious experience – initially diffuse in the poetry of
the Upanishads, and gradually condensed later in the com-
mentaries of the Vedanta – which, right up to the present day,
has continually sought embodiment in a complex series of
monist philosophies: while at the same time, through an
accompanying exaggeration of the feeling of the 'unreality of
phenomena', Buddhism was being born, causing a large proportion of mystical energies to evaporate in 'the intoxication
of emptiness'.

b. In sharp contrast to this theist and pantheist attitude,
China emerges from the very beginning as fundamentally
naturistic and humanist. Whether we look at Taoism, which
explains the universe metaphysically by a theory of contraries,
or at Confucianist wisdom, which is based empirically on
tradition handed down by ancestors, Chinese thought is
dominated throughout its whole history by an ever-present
sense of the *primacy of the tangible* in relation to the invisible.
The supreme being, it is true, is not excluded from this mental

climate (we have only to remember the Temple of Heaven), but he is to an alarming degree assimilated to the firmament. The same is true of spirit, also, which is too readily identified with material currents of air and water. Here we have a concept of the supernatural which veers towards geomancy; a passion for ideas diverted into the cult of calligraphy; an ethical system concerned mainly with practical morality; and finally a Buddhism (the Buddhism which China received from India) which substitutes for the Nirvana the attractive, compassionate, and so human figure of Amida: all these are signs which characterize and reveal in the Chinese a persistent and ultimately always victorious predilection for man and the earth.

c. When we move on to Japan, we find a third habit of mind. It is again a form of humanism; but it is very different from, or even the very converse of, what we found in China; in this sense, that the individual is no longer the centre of society, but its servant. For a complex variety of reasons, partly some racial psychism, partly the country's warlike history and geographical isolation, the Japanese seems to have a stronger innate feeling for the life of the clan than for his own. This accounts for his warrior-mysticism, in which, as René Grousset points out, Buddhist renunciation and anti-realism (first adapted by the Chinese to satisfy their innate feeling for the concrete) are here reformulated, through Zen, into a code of chivalrous violence and self-sacrifice.

In India, then, we find a metaphysical sense of the divine; in China, a naturistic and practical sense of the human; in Japan, an heroic sense of the collective. And so the allegedly simple light we are urged to seek again from the Far East breaks down under analysis into three groups of completely different shades. In fact – whether by some hidden harmony in things, or by mere coincidence – these three groups are oddly complementary. Taken together, indeed, do they not exactly cover the complete field of a perfect spirituality? Mysticism of God, mysticism of the individual confronted by the world, social mysticism: there you have the complete picture. There is this, however, to be noted: these three components of a complete life of the spirit are dispersed, ethnically and geographically, over three different areas of the continent; and not only do we not find them in eastern Asia except in a disparate form, but, what is more, when we come to look at them more closely we find that they possess characteristics which make them (at least for the time being, in their present form) mutually exclusive and irreconcilable.

II. FORMULATIONS OF SPIRITUALITY IN THE FAR EAST

Let us now resume, but this time more analytically, our examination of the spiritual currents of the Far East. Let us repeat our tour of India, China, and Japan, but this time with an eye to apprehending and defining, not so much in its general tendencies as in its specific expression, what one might call the 'soul' of each of the three human groups under consideration. What does such an examination tell us?

a. Although we find in Indian systems an extreme polymorphism which lends itself to all sorts of deceptive kinship with Western thought, the religious metaphysics of India appears undoubtedly to be governed, in its essence and its very fabric, by a *very particular concept of unity*; and this, if I am not mistaken, gives Hindu 'theism', in whatever form it may be expressed, a colouring and flavour that are immediately recognizable. To overcome the harrowing multiplicity of the world in which we are immersed – to arrive at some beatifying unity – such is the basic dream, more or less explicit as the case may be, of *all* human mysticism, throughout all time and in all countries. The problem, however, is to know what road to follow if this fundamental and vital process of cosmic unification is to be effected. Later I shall be referring to what I call the 'road of the West'. In the East, by which I mean India, the instinctive, innate, unquestioned solution to the problem seems always to have been as follows.

'If (as is infinitely desirable) we are to unify the multiple, whether in our own selves or in the world around us, there is no more radical nor more simple plan than to deny it or suppress it. You dream of hearing the resonance of the fundamental note? Then be silent. You seek to emerge from turmoil and the plural? Then gradually make your way down into the depths of your own self, blotting out one by one all the tints – iridescent or over-harsh – into which being is broken down, to form the apparent reality of the world around you: and when you have descended to the very bottom, *below every conceivable determination*, you will find that a universal essence lies at that term, *underlying* everything, and that it is waiting only for you to return to it to absorb and *identify* you with itself.'

So we have a sort of God-substratum, or again a 'God of non-tension', attained by relaxation of the effort towards differentiation in which the cosmic phenomenon involves us: it is basically that object, and expressed in those sorts of terms, which Hindu wisdom offers, in countless different forms, to our need to worship. In the final reckoning, there is no true love in this attitude: *for identification is not union.*[1] Nor is there any room for humanism in the sense in which our generation understands the word; for no essential value is attributed in this view to the planetary constructions of human effort.[2] Keeping this second point well in mind, let us now turn to China.

b. If India, by nature, is bathed in an atmosphere of the transcendent and the divine, China, as we saw earlier, is above all, and always has been, a focus of material and human aspirations. But, as this earthly flower has blossomed, what particular design has it disclosed, what brilliance, what special savour has it chiefly developed? If it be possible and permissible to condense into a cut-and-dried formula the exuberant reality spread over three thousand years of practical good living, of art and poetry, might we not say – in fact, must we not say – that what characterizes the soul of ancient China is *appreciation* of man, much more than *faith* in man? China, it is true, has not remained completely static throughout its history; but it would not appear to have concerned itself greatly with the onward drive the movement embodies. To perceive, to appreciate and to preserve the harmony of an established order – to effect a fine and stable balance between the earth, society and the stars – to pacify rather than to conquer – such would appear to have been China's predominant concern and the source of her loftiest

[1]This was clearly understood in the eighth century by the advocates of Bhakti Yoga. But the mode of union proposed by this yoga (or Hindu mysticism) of love is surely of the Western type (see below) and therefore incompatible with the original and authentic tendencies of the Vedanta.

[2]In 1946, during an interview with Siddheswarananda, who represented the Ramakrishna mission, Père Teilhard was at pains to obtain more accurate information about the various forms of yoga, and to confirm that in India the highest ecstasy corresponded to final loss of consciousness in an impersonal whole. (Ed.)

aspirations. And the inevitable result of this was that, even if heaven was always there to form a roof over the city of man, its vault was nevertheless regarded as impenetrable; and nothing in the way of progress for life was envisaged which might arouse the desire or hope of ever penetrating it. Take what you have, and dispose it accordingly. Neither the spirit of Prometheus nor the problem of action ever seems to have haunted or disturbed the soul of Confucius or Lao-Tse. Here we find a form of wisdom which certainly moved at a higher level than the world, but which, by suppressing in logic if not in fact all anxiety for, all the demands of, the future, tended to weaken the whole drive towards, to cut every road leading to, what during the same period was India's sole and burning desire: the transcendent.

c. Finally, let us look once more at Japan. Here it is no longer movement that is lacking, nor the spirit of conquest; it is much more the general organic structure capable of using and sublimating this magnificent source of energy. Historically, the Japanese soul seems to have expressed itself in too narrow a framework, race and the racial spirit: race centred on blood and common origin much more than on spirit and convergence ahead; and racial spirit doubly dehumanized in as much as, by improperly retaining the biological conditions of the animal 'phylum' at the level of reflective life, it resists the convergence of human filiations, and, within each filiation, tends to keep each individual in the condition of a mere link. This gives rise to an exclusive, closed mysticism, equally impenetrable, in its practical spirit of service and sacrifice, to the supreme detachment of the Hindu and the supreme good sense of the Chinese.

So we reach the conclusion I suggested when we started. God and his transcendence; the world and its value; the individual and the importance of the person: mankind and social requirements: taken in isolation, each of these great problems has indeed been seen and attacked by the East – always, however, leading in the end to a series of particular and mutually incompatible solutions. The East has not solved the problem of spirit, taken in its complete totality; and we would look in vain in that quarter for the dawn to illuminate it. Should we not, then, turn back to the West and ask ourselves whether it may not perhaps be on our side that the sun will this time rise?

III. THE ROAD OF THE WEST

As I pointed out when I began, the European is not regarded as being either by temperament or by his inventions, a religious being. Reason dries up in him the well of fancy, and he is entirely absorbed in material structures: such is his reputation. In defiance of this preconceived judgement, I maintain, and I hope to demonstrate here, that underlying the creative fever of the West, and combined with it, there is a true mystical ferment, the fruit of Christianity and a new humanism. It is a young mysticism, original and powerful, still perhaps clumsily constructed and ill-expressed in its theory, but perfectly defined in its main lines, and the hidden inspiration of the whole 'modern' movement.

Let us, then, try to define this mysticism and bring it out into the open.

If we look deep into Western man, we meet again, of course, the operation of that fundamental aspiration or anxiety, which, as I pointed out earlier, drives all reflective consciousness in the direction of an increasing unity; but we find, at the same time, the outline of a new and hitherto untried solution to this primordial need of every age. 'In order to become one with all', is the constant message of one part of the East, 'suppress the plurality of the phenomenon.' 'If you wish to become one with all,' is the contrary decision of the West, 'resolutely embrace the multiple, and urge it with all your energies in the direction in which it tends, through a bias proper to it, to develop organic structure and to *converge* upon itself.' This is a slow and laborious process. It calls for a constant effort to rise higher, to leave behind, to pass through. But it works. And because it replaces immersion in a substratum-God, a God of non-tension, by the anticipation of a God who is centre and peak, a God who is tension, it immediately establishes complete coherence between the different spiritual values which the wisdom of the East found it impossible to reconcile.

Governing the whole picture in the first place, the absolute necessity of a divine principle is evident, since it is that existence and that alone which can provide the universe, outside time and space, with a transcendent point of attraction, of convergence, and of irreversible consolidation: God, the prime psychic mover ahead.

At the same time, too, the value of human effort, including even man's most material activities, is seen to be justified and hallowed: because (precisely as a result of the convergent mechanism of union) the consummation of unity implies structurally – not, indeed, as a sufficient, but as a necessary condition – the loyalty with which the world will actively use all the support it finds in the spring-board of matter, to raise itself to its highest possible degree of organic structure and deter-mination.

Thereby, too, love regains its dignity as the supreme spiritual energy, and at the same time the human person has its irre-placeable and incommunicable essence restored: for, since the process of unification culminates in an act not of identification but of *union*, the elements involved in the operation are not dissolved by their entry into God, but are continually more super-centred upon themselves.

And yet in this system full allowance is made for the opera-tion and requirements of collective forces, since it is exclusively through 'unanimization' that the elements of the universe – by reason of its convergent structure – can hope to attain the pole of their personality and their reflection.

Looked at in this way, we must admit that all the major data of the spiritual problem are readily organized into an harmonious and fruitful whole. On the rational side, the con-tradictions disappear; and an immensely wide field is opened up for the directionally controlled operation of the most elevated forms of action.

Here it is important to understand exactly what I mean. I am not saying of the philosophico-mystical choice whose starting point and further developments I have just broadly indicated that it has yet found in the West its clear, undisputed and indisputable expression. What I do maintain is that the Western choice, on careful and sympathetic consideration (or analysis of the psyche), so colours and dominates every one of our fundamental reactions to life[3] that no great perspicacity is needed to see that at this moment the West is the starting point

[3]Including even, paradoxical though this may seem, 'Marxist' aspirations: which to me are no more than Western mysticism unwarrantably limited to that branch of it or, one might say, that central focus) which looks to material organization.

143

for an advance, a general breakthrough, of spirit in the direction I have indicated.

How, indeed, could it be otherwise?

At other periods of history, it may well be that man's inventive genius has been shared (one might say) between various ethnic groups, each group possessing special capabilities for a particular line of progress: in one case, art; in another, the sciences; in another, religion or metaphysics, and so on. At our present stage in anthropogenesis, there would certainly appear to be a sort of mobilization or concentration at work within man's powers of discovery. It is becoming more and more impossible for any step in material organization to be taken on this earth which does not *there and then* call for an equivalent step in the psychic and spiritual domain, to balance, humanize and complete it. In a world which is becoming totalized (or even 'cephalized'), the two movements are coalescing into one. That is why the West could not at this moment be (as it undoubtedly is) the spearhead of science, nor retain its position as such, were it not at the same time the shaft, too, of religious creative effort. Today, in fact, all eyes are instinctively turned towards us, to see not only how to build but also how to believe. Underestimating its own capabilities, Europe is hesitating; it is looking to Asia, with a plea for wisdom – and yet, even in that field, it is Asia that is turning to us.

I shall be told that this is an exaggeration: and yet, consider, in India, the humanism of a Tagore. Go further East, and follow the astonishing, irresistible movement that is taking place in China: suddenly converting into a completely modern faith in man the ancient, traditional appreciation of man, it is successfully turning the humblest Chinese peasant into a death-defying proselyte. Note, as I have been able to do, the way in which the best Japanese thinkers are gradually widening their native clan-centred ambitions to a global scale.

Surely all these indications point to the fact, if they do not amount to a proof of it, that the East is yielding from within to an emancipating instinct, and slowly getting under way with its whole spiritual mass, to join up, not only technologically but mystically too, with the road of the West.

IV. THE CONFLUENCE OF EAST AND WEST

'The whole spiritual mass of the East once more under way': I would like to conclude the evidence offered here with that great possibility or even, I would say – if my judgement is correct – that great event.

An ever-increasing number of persons is concerned with this much canvassed question of a convergence of East and West; they are apt to picture it to themselves by the idea of two complementary blocs, or two conflicting principles, which are merging into one: another example of Chinese Tao's *yin* and *yang*. To my mind, if the meeting is effected – as sooner or later *must* happen – the phenomenon will come about as the result of a different mechanism, one much more akin to that by which a number of streams pour simultaneously through a breach opened by one of them in a common retaining barrier.

As it happens, and through a complex of historical factors which it would not be difficult to analyse, the honour and the opportunity of opening the road for a new surge of human consciousness have fallen, I repeat, to the West. But while there can no longer be any doubt about the correct approach, or even about whether the breach has been made, we are still a long way from the final target; nor can we be certain of success. In one sense, the real battle for spirit is only beginning in our world; and if we are to win it, all the available forces must be brought into action.

So far, as I have tried to show, the three main spiritual currents of the Far East have not yet found their point of confluence nor, in consequence, their complete expression. Their waters have been rising silently in enclosed lakes. Yet I am sure that the time is approaching when their massive reserves will pour through the gap made by Europe's penetrating tenacity and be incorporated in ours. For a long time now, the Eastern soul (Hindu, Chinese, or Japanese), each following its own specially favoured line and in its own special way, has had the answer to the religious aspirations whose pole of convergence and whose laws we, in the West, are now engaged in determining more exactly: that answer is no doubt less clear than ours and less of a synthesis, but it has, possibly, a deeper innate foundation, and greater vigour. And what results may we not expect when the confluence is at last effected? In the first place, there will be the quantitative influx of a vast human flood now waiting to be used; but, what is even more valuable, there will be the qualitative enrichment produced by the coming together of different psychic essences and different temperaments.

In every domain of thought, whether religious or scientific, it is only in union with all other men that each individual man can hope to reach what is most ultimate and profound in his own being. By this I do not mean that we have to be initiated into a higher form of spirit, but rather that, forming a new resonant whole, we must add volume and richness to the new (the humano-Christian) mystical note rising from the

West. Such, in a word, I believe to be the indispensable role and the essential function at the present moment of the Far East.

10 February 1947

TWO PRINCIPLES AND
A COROLLARY
(OR A *WELTANSCHAUUNG*
IN THREE STAGES)

Introduction

In conformity with what we may call the 'law of complexity-consciousness', there is at the moment a rapid rise in the psychic temperature on earth, caused by the activity of an economico-technological network which is being tightened at a continually accelerated speed. And it is equally clear, on the other hand, that the first effect of this rise is to produce within the thinking envelope represented by man a state of turbulence which our generation finds most disconcerting. From every quarter, as though we were at the centre of a cyclone, waves of mutually hostile ideas are rearing themselves up and clashing together: evolutionism and fixism – Christianity and Marxism – so many different answers with which our mind reacts to the ever-increasing pressure exerted on it by the double question of the *meaning* and the *value* of the world around us.

To the reflective element which each one of us constitutes, there seems at first sight to be no decisive way of finding our bearings and determining our direction in this orderless turmoil. And yet, if we only believe in the viability of the human type, surely everything goes to show that the chaos in which we are involved is no more than temporary: a mere phase, only to be expected, of interference and adjustment between old currents and new currents – the broken water of their superficial conflict is only the prelude to the deeper harmony of some powerful underlying flow.

What I wish to show in this essay is that such a hope is not only permissible, but rests on a solid foundation: and this not by invoking abstract considerations, arguing a priori, but with the support of concrete examples. By this I mean explaining the way in which, to my mind, a simple and consistent line of advance (one that completely satisfies the demands, and is commensurate with the powers of human action) is being marked out for us at the very centre of the spiritual storm in which we are enveloped – provided, however, that we obey what the facts suggest, and, disregarding all preconceptions to the contrary, we resolutely extend to their furthest limit two judgements of value. The first is purely rational and relates to the biological nature of the social phenomenon; the second is specifically Christian, and relates to the physical basis of the parousia. Let me try to explain how this may be done.

I. FIRST JUDGEMENT OF VALUE: IN ITS EVOLUTION, MANKIND IS MAKING A FRESH LEAP, UNDER THE IMPULSE OF A COLLECTIVE DRIVE, TOWARDS A STILL-TO-COME MATURATION-POINT

Understanding of this first fundamental point presupposes the acceptance of three basic choices, the justification of which, and their logical connection, I have explained elsewhere.[1]

Here I give a brief summary of what I then wrote.

a. *Choice 1.* Life is neither an accident, nor an incident, in

[1]'Turmoil or genesis? Is there in the universe a main axis of evolution?' (December 1947) in *The Future of Man* (Collins, London, and Harper & Row, New York, 1964), p. 214; Fontana edition (London, 1969), p. 222.

the material universe. It shows, carried to its highest observable degree, a general process of involution (at once quantitative and qualitative) through which a sort of amorphous primordial cosmic stuff has continually, it would appear, been concentrating upon itself a multitude of ever more complex corpuscles:[2] the phenomenon of 'consciousness', when looked at from this angle, being simply the specific property of a matter which has been taken to extreme states of complexity. And in this connection, moreover, it is of no importance whether the phenomenon first originates as an effect of condensation (the universe of Laplace) or explosion (the expanding universe).

b. *Choice 2.* Within the living world, human psychism is not a mere variety of consciousness, one among thousands of others – nor is it a monstrous anomaly. It corresponds to the emergence, or the development, in a domain *of a higher order* (the domain of reflection) of a certain specially favoured psychic radiation. With man, it is life itself that attains a *new state*, characterized, among other things, by the two properties of *prevision* and *deliberate invention*.

c. *Choice 3.* Finally, within mankind, each individual reflective centre (the 'person') does not represent the upper limit of cosmic involution known to our experience. On the contrary, examination of the social phenomenon (technological superarrangement of individuals, accompanied by intensification of consciousness – cf. Introduction), seems to point to the con-

---

[2]The process would appear, in reality, to be made up of two inverse involutions: one starts from the immensely large and divides the stuff of the cosmos 'aggregatively' into continually smaller fragments (stellar involution – from nebulae to planets); the other starts in the infinitesimal and produces (through structural complexity) continually larger corpuscles (atomic involution – from atoms to living creatures and man). Both involutions (stellar and atomic) meet in the case of the human noosphere, in which the organic mega-corpuscle (mankind) becomes co-extensive with its astral support (the earth). Here we are directly concerned only with atomic involution.

clusion that the process of centration from which each one of us has emerged is being extended on a global scale at a higher level – each elementary human *vortex* continuing to be concentrated upon itself only within and under the pressure of a *more general vortex* which is folding back into itself the totality of mankind.

I do not believe that any real observer of the world and life can today entertain any serious doubt about the actual reality of man's social super-humanization within mankind: in other words he must accept the validity of the three inter-dependent choices of which I have just spoken. On the other hand, it would not appear that biologists have as yet thought it either profitable or possible to define more closely their views on the nature and limits of this 'eighth act' in the drama of creation. They either leave the configuration of the cosmic future of spirit completely indeterminate; or, in order to ensure for it that perennial, 'limitless' quality which we cannot deny to it without destroying our own most deeply implanted zest for living, there is a vague acceptance (J. B. S. Haldane is an example) of a wave of thought which radiates from the earth and gradually (either alone or in combination with other similar waves) penetrates the totality of space.

And yet, if we pursue to its logical conclusion the hypothesis, accepted here as a guide, of a universe in process of involution, surely it points to a much less fanciful and much more precise picture of the future. I must emphasize this again: if it is indeed true that men – both as one whole, and each on his own account – reach the term of their individual re-involution through collective envelopment in a vast maelstrom, then there is no need to look for the extensions of anthropogenesis in the direction of a cosmic diffusion. In virtue of its structure, we have admitted, super-hominization is a closed process; we must therefore try to express its supreme culmination in terms not of divergence, but of convergence. No: whatever may be the effects of 'planetary expansion' that astronautics has in store for us, the main part of the human phenomenon is developing in the direction not of an indefinitely continued expansion, but in the opposite direction of a centration.

It is this that prompts the idea, suggested and accepted here as being the most consistent – or even, perhaps, as being alone consistent – with the sum total of our knowledge, of a point of *maturation*, which lies at the term of the earth's biological evolution, in other words of noogenesis.

Looked at from this angle, we see how mankind's strict association with his planetary support must persist until its very end, and how man might end his existence on it (or, more correctly, might be detached from it), not under the impact of an external catastrophe, nor as the result of some internal malady or exhaustion – but by arrival at a certain critical state of metamorphosis (a combination of the highest psychic tension with the highest technological organization), beyond which we can distinguish nothing in the future: and the reason for our inability is precisely that what is involved is a 'critical point' of emergence (we might almost use the astronomers' 'emersion') from the universe's temporo-spatial matrix.[3]

[3]This point of human maturation may be defined psychologically as a point of 'general reflection' which corresponds to a certain optimum of reflection produced in all the mutually reflected terrestrial elements: and this means, as I have said elsewhere, that man's historical evolution would appear to be effected between two critical points of reflection (one, lower and individual; the other, higher and collective). Such an ontological phenomenon cannot, however, be conceived without the accompanying production, in the 'cognitive' and 'affective' order, of some general *Weltanschauung* in which minds find a common basis on which to support their common reflection. What is more – and this is implied in the very notion of a critical point – this must

This view, let me repeat, is perfectly consistent (or even 'is alone consistent') with the plan of physico-psychic involution found in the world. What I wish now to show is how remarkably it is in harmony with the design which is most essential both to Revelation and to the hopes entertained by Christians.

II. SECOND JUDGEMENT OF VALUE: AS A CONCRETE FACT, THE HUMAN MATURATION-POINT, DEFINED ABOVE, COINCIDES WITH WHAT WE KNOW AS THE POINT OF 'CHRISTIC PAROUSIA'

The parousia (or Christ's return in glory at the end of all time) occupies a central position in the firmament of the Christian world – even though long centuries of continued waiting have made it easy to forget. It is in this unique and supreme event, in which (so faith tells us) the historic is to be fused in the transcendent, that the mystery of the Incarnation culminates: and this asserts itself with all the realism of a physical explanation of the universe. No believer doubts the sheer actuality of the fact: the problem is how to picture it to ourselves.

So far, for reasons that derive from Scripture, from tradition, and from instinct, the end of the world and the last judgement have mostly been interpreted and expressed (for does not a sudden transformation always take on the appearance of an

---

take place in an atmosphere not of relaxation and tranquillity, but of tension and ebullition. (Cf. below.)

We should note incidentally that initially (i.e. before any further reflection *per descensum*) the cosmogenic design suggested here does not introduce any *finality*, or any *orthogenesis*, other than that which can exist, and which everyone accepts without hesitation, in the course of a river or the formation of a whirlpool. The only difference is that the stream with whose stirring into motion we are here concerned is not a mass of water or galactic substance: it is the whole of the stuff of the cosmos in process of total, multi-centric re-involution upon itself.

accident?) as some form of catastrophe; but if we follow this apocalyptic line, we should realize that we must advance with caution. All recent progress in exegesis is a warning that while Revelation guides our steps, on the other hand it cannot *describe* to us the point from which we start, nor the point at which we are going to arrive: it is no more 'prophetic' about the great expanse of the future than it is about that of the past. In these matters, which transcend experience, only an essential nucleus of truth, underlying any form in which they are represented, is to be retained: and in the case of the parousia this would seem to be reducible to the three following elements – – a crisis, a concentration, and finally (under Christic influence) a spiritualizing consummation in some human super-organism. And so we see that precisely in virtue of these three characteristic elements, the road of religion leads us back to the same *general type* of event as that which (as we have just explained) might be theoretically anticipated by our reason as the biological term of hominization. In both cases, may we not be concerned, fundamentally, with one and the same thing?

From this we derive the following hypothesis: for all its simplicity, it is pillar 'no. 2' supporting the general picture I am describing here.

For Christ to appear on earth for the first time it was obviously necessary (as no one would question) that, following the general process of evolution, the human type should be anatomically developed, and socially advanced, up to a certain degree of collective consciousness. That being so, why should we not take a further step, and believe that in the case of his second and final coming *too*, Christ is waiting to reappear until the human collectivity has at last become capable (because fully realized in its natural potentialities) of receiving from him its supernatural consummation? After all, if there are without doubt exact physical laws for the development of spirit within history, why should there not be, *a fortiori*, laws for its further expansion and ultimate consummation?

Let us then, accepting this idea, posit a coincidence between Christic parousia-point and human maturation-point, at different levels but within the concrete unity of one and the same event. In other words, let us say that since the latter is a condition of the former (not, of course, sufficient and determining, but necessary), the two cannot but be produced simultaneously. What follows from this identification, or to put it more exactly, this conjunction?

In the first place, no important change is introduced into the traditional Christian way of envisaging the end of all time. For (and this is a point which must be stressed) while Scripture warns us emphatically of a crisis which will be final and unexpected, nothing could be less peaceful, nothing more 'critical', and, up to a point, nothing more impossible to foresee, than the focal centre on which, concentrating at a higher level than ourselves, man's social involution is converging.

Moreover, in the prospect which my view opens up, there is nothing which opens the door to unwarranted reconciliation of incompatibles. It does not involve deceptive assimilations of fragments of truth taken from different planes of knowledge, but simply a 'polar' convergence of two lines of vision (one biological, the other mystical) which agree on the general form of equilibrium (or super-union) that may be expected from a pluralist world in process of unification.

Thus, there is no serious disadvantage in what I suggest. And, on the other hand, there is what we still have to see – the truly remarkable rise of spiritual energy at the heart of the universe thus 'mono-cephalized'.[4]

III. THIRD POINT OR COROLLARY: A NEW PSYCHIC ENERGY AVAILABLE TO NOOGENESIS. THE PROBLEM, AND THE SYNTHESIS OF THE TWO FAITHS[5]

If I am not mistaken, we would be justified in saying that the root source of the spiritual troubles in which mankind is struggling today is what may be called 'the conflict of the two faiths'.

Until about the time of the Renaissance, it still seemed as though the whole earth, following in the steps of the West, must gradually allow itself to be taken over and exalted by the ascensional force of Christianity: in a striving for mere detachment which would be a continuation – corrected, personalized, and 'Mediterraneanized' – of a mystical tendency that had long been familiar to the peoples of the East. Saint and sage were agreed that there was, for man, but one issue open to the world: an upward issue, sheer or modified, from matter.

Starting with the Renaissance, however, another tendency was born deep in the mind of man: at first it was not easy to detect, but with the nineteenth century it was asserting itself ever more rapidly. In a vague way, man had always felt (witness Babel, the Titans, Prometheus) that he had wings, *his own* wings, and that the day would come when he would develop his own power of flight. But it is only quite recently, and as collective organization of his energies taught him his own

---

[4]The whole picture described here could be expressed in logical sequence by the following series of equations: Cosmos = cosmogenesis = biogenesis = individual anthropogenesis = collective anthropogenesis = Christogenesis.

[5]Père Teilhard adds the English 'faiths' to the French 'fois'. (Ed.)

capacity for self-evolution, that this primordial feeling of power has begun to become in man a normal, hereditary and generalized habit of mind. Not to see this today would argue complete blindness to facts. Another type of faith is coming to challenge the old traditional faith (divine faith) in a Transcendent, lying above: it is a new faith, a human faith in some Immanent, lying ahead.[6] Just as happens in a crowd when some new exit is opened to the stream of people, so a vast eddy is being formed at the heart of the human mass; and this is carrying it no longer towards heaven, but towards some great but as yet ill-defined terrestrial future. Initially, it might well seem as though the two currents were mutually irreconcilable and contradictory. Is it not two camps, two psychological species, in fact, that are emerging in our world of today? On the one side the spiritualists (above all Christian) whose faith in God seems to make them immune from all hope, all desire, for the appearance of super-mankind. And on the other side are the materialists (above all Marxists), who regard every allowance made to the Transcendent and to finality of purpose as a compromising and a dilution of their faith in man.

It is precisely in this disturbing conflict that the coincidence noted above between human maturation-point and Christic parousia-point intervenes, and acts as a releasing agent. Parousia-point: the culmination of Christian faith. Maturation-point: the peak of human faith. If these two focal centres, these two stars, coincide, how can the least opposition persist between the tides produced by their gravitational pull? And how even, one may well ask with astonishment, has it ever been possible to see opposition where there is nothing but two components,

[6] Is it not in fact the second of these two currents which is at this moment proving the most lively, the most infectiously influential, and the most productive of the spirit of sacrifice?

each equally anxious to come together in a common resultant? Unfortunately there are, as we were saying, many Christians to whom the very idea of earthly progress still seems a temptation of the devil:[7] they regard it as a forbidden fruit. But I wonder whether these timid believers ever suspect what treasures of man's vital energy, what precious 'tangibility' of support for spiritual effort, they are denying themselves, simply from failing to understand a very simple and very important fact: that man cannot hope to meet Christ 'supernaturally' without at the same time (or, indeed, without first) arriving in his own nature at the furthest limit of his human self? What is more, how can these same men still call themselves Christians, when they deliberately seek to exclude from their concern and their field of influence ambitions and dreams that have now arrived permanently as the newest and most vital ingredient in the modern soul?

There is also, I added, the mass of new believers in mankind, for whom the gospel is no more than a dangerous opiate. These, too, must surely realize that without Christianity the world becomes a place in which, in a twofold sense, it is impossible for man to breathe. First, because such a world is heartbreakingly barred ahead, confronted by total death. And secondly, because it no longer contains any living warmth to animate its terrifying mechanism.

Working on its own, the elevating force of Christianity might well lose its vigour and disappear; while, to balance this, if man's propulsive force is left to itself it still lacks (and these are fatal deficiencies) any factor that makes for irreversibility and personalization.

[7] A legacy, no doubt, from the time when the idea of anthropogenesis had not yet been conceived – or from a still earlier (proto-historic) time when the demiurge could still be regarded as suspicious and jealous of the power developed by his own creation.

On the other hand, once the two tendencies come together and are combined in one and the same consciousness (as the concrete identity of their respective centres of effort and attraction makes possible, or, rather, makes inevitable), then we see that an astonishing, dual, psychic event can, and indeed must occur: and this comes about not merely by an intellectual identification, but by a real confluence, of the two most powerful spiritual currents we can now distinguish in mankind – one driving towards what lies above, the other towards what lies ahead.

The first of these is the appearance[8] in the soul of man of a new sort of faith ('super-humanized' Christian faith), more powerful than any other, and therefore destined sooner or later to prevail, with absolute certainty, over all the others.

And the second is the possibility for the Christian (by reason of the identification effected between anthropogenesis and Christogenesis) not only of recognizing and serving evolution, but also of literally – and in a higher meaning of the word – *loving* it.

The emergence of so astonishingly rich and so completely new a mental condition might at first be taken to be no more than the attainment by the individual of an interior mystical plenitude.

In real fact, the repercussions of the phenomenon are much more far-reaching, and much more important.

By this I mean that the more we consider the extreme complexity of the planetary organism that man, if he is to consummate man, finds himself obliged to achieve, the stronger our conviction that there is only one way in which the 'motor'

[8]In logic, and therefore in fact: for in the end it is always the 'psychically' stronger that wins.

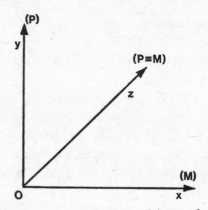

Diagrammatic representation of the two faiths

Oy = Christianity's ascensional force towards a Transcendent. Faith in God

Ox = Human propulsive force towards an Immanent lying ahead. Faith in man

Oz = Resultant: 'Super-humanized' Christian faith

 P = Parousia-point

 M = Human maturation-point

Oz   combines the properties of Ox (influx of human vital energy, tangibility) and of Oy (irreversibility, warmth) - and makes a 'love of evolution' possible.

required for such a purpose can operate: it cannot do so without distorting the free elements of which it is composed, nor, what is more, can it release the hidden reserves of their spiritual powers, unless the force applied to it be *affectivo-unitive* in nature. Biologically, in the case of a personalizing totalization - which is what the formation of a noosphere gives us - love (a universal love) is the only conceivable form that can be taken by a truly evolutive energy.

And this leads me to my final remark: in the dual intellectual event (by which I mean the gradual appearance in the field of

TWO PRINCIPLES AND A COROLLARY

human consciousness of a maturation-point, combined with progressive identification, in the field of Christian consciousness, of the 'general reflection-point' with the parousia) – in this dual event which makes possible the birth of such a love, we should not see a mere chance encounter. What in fact happens is precisely as though, as a result of this coincidence, life were developing, just at the right moment, the exact environment, the exact spiritual temperature, that are essential to it if it is still to continue its self-involution.[9]

Paris, February 1948

[9]From this point of view, noospheric maturation (being linked to a dynamized form of charity) cannot be effected without the Church's animating action making itself more strongly felt at the heart of mankind. And this amounts to the eminently satisfying proposition that terrestrial progress will attain the 'parousiac flash-point' only on condition of, and through the agency of, its own internal self-Christification.

LETTER FROM PÈRE TEILHARD DE CHARDIN
TO MLLE JEANNE MORTIER CONCERNING
'MY FUNDAMENTAL VISION'

Thank you for your kind letter of the 20th which arrived only yesterday in this remote corner. I think you are probably over-generous in your praise of Comment je Vois *('My Fundamental Vision'); but I am glad, anyway, that you were favourably impressed. As I told you, there can as yet be no question of printing such an essay: it is addressed to the professional. Nevertheless, your comments are justified – at least the majority of them. On p. 26[1] I see no reason for changing* forcément *('perforce') unless you would prefer* inévitablement – *which is not quite so strong: I am not saying that God must in any case immerse himself – but only that if he wishes to create, he must immerse himself. And that certainly does not over-step the bounds of classic orthodoxy. Page 25[2]: here the difficulty is more serious, and so what I had in mind was to indicate certain lines (in the form of the note or elucidation added at the end of the piece) as an aid to determining more exactly the relationship between the two ideas of* being *and* union.

Les Moulins, Neuville, Puy-de-Dôme,
24 August 1948

[1]p. 196 of the following text.
[2]p. 194 of the following text.

MY FUNDAMENTAL VISION

Introductory note

Part 1. PHYSICS (Phenomenology)
  I. The Phenomenon of Man
    1. The involuting universe, or the cosmic primacy of life
    2. Elementary hominization, or the breakthrough into reflection
    3. Collective humanization, or the advance into super-reflection
    4. The orientation of the future, and Omega Point
  II. The Christian Phenomenon

Part 2: METAPHYSICS

Part 3: MYSTICISM

Conclusion

Appendix

'It seems to me that a whole life-time of continual hard work would be as nothing to me, if only I could, just for one moment, give a true picture of what I see.'

What follows is divided into thirty-eight paragraphs, arranged in three chapters (a 'physics', or phenomenology, a metaphysics, and a mysticism), and it contains, in the form of a connected argument, the whole body of scientific and parascientific views whose progressive elaboration has been the object of my earlier essays. Here will be found – to be endorsed or criticized – an authentic and complete summary of my present intellectual attitude to the world and to God – the essence of my faith. And because I know in advance that the chief objection I shall meet will be, 'All this is too simple and too delightful to be true', I feel that I must, before I begin, make these three remarks, or, rather, put forward these three affirmations:

1. First, in spite of certain appearances to the contrary, the '*Weltanschauung*' I offer in no way represents a fixed and closed system. There is no question here (for such a thing would be absurd) of a deductive *solution* to the world, in the manner of Hegel, of a definitive framework of truth – it is simply a cluster of axial lines of progression, such as exists and gradually comes to light in every evolutionary system. There is no exhaustive presentation of truth; there are simply lines of penetration through which we can see a still unexplored immensity of the real opening up for us.

2. Secondly (and here I am answering an objection that has already been made), we must be careful not to confuse 'concordism' with 'coherence'. We are all familiar, in the history of ideas, with certain infantile, over-hasty reconciliations, which fail to distinguish between planes and sources of knowledge, and so produce constructions which can only be unstable, because grotesque; but such exaggeratedly forced harmonizations should not make us forget that the essential criterion of truth, its specific mark, is its power of developing indefinitely – not only without ever producing internal contradiction, but also in such a way as to form a positively constructed whole in which the parts support and complement one another ever more effectively. At the equator, it would be ridiculous (and this is concordism) to confuse meridians on a sphere: but (and this is coherence) structural necessity demands that these same meridians meet together at the pole.

3. A fundamental implication of all this is my third postulate, which is in line with all that is closest to the heart of Greek and Mediterranean tradition: that the conscious takes precedence of the unconscious, and the reflective of the instinctive; consciousness and reflection never exhaust the psychic reserves they organize according to a design which is based on a centre; it is in their direction, in the direction of consciousness and reflection, that life's current always flows, so that one may say that, for the stuff of the cosmos, its higher form of existence and its final state of equilibrium is in *being thought*.[1]

---

[1]'Everything seeks to be thought' (Charles de Bouvelles, quoted by Bernard Groethuysen, in *Mesures*, 16 January 1940).

1. Physics (Phenomenology)

I. THE PHENOMENON OF MAN

1. *The involuting universe, or the cosmic primacy of life*

1. In the construction of systems of physics, it has always been the case until now that only a single axis in the world has been taken into consideration: that axis which runs through magnitudes of the middle order (in which we are physically included), rising from the extremely small towards the extremely large, from the infinitesimal to the immense. Physics still confines itself to only two 'infinites'. And yet this is not enough. If the totality of experience is to be covered scientifically, then it is necessary, I believe, to take into consideration a further 'infinite' in the universe, one that is no less real than the other two: the infinite, I mean, of complexity. The bodies among which we move are not only large or small; they are also simple or complex. And, expressed numerically – crude though the approximation must be – simply by the number of elements in combination, the gap between the extreme of simplicity and the extreme of complexity is as astronomically great as that between stellar and atomic magnitudes. It is therefore in a very strict sense, and by no means metaphorically, that the scientist can speak of a 'third infinite', which, starting from the infinitesimal, builds up in the immense, at the level of the middle order. And this third, as I said before, is the infinite of complexity.

2. The effect of introducing the complexities-axis into our fundamental scheme of the universe is not confined simply to

including more explicitly, and without distortion, a larger section of the experiential world. The most important result of the change is that it makes it easy to connect the phenomena of life – consciousness, freedom, inventive power – to the phenomena of matter: in other words, to find a natural place for biology as part of physics. If, in fact, as universal experience shows us, life represents a controlled whole of properties that appear and develop as a function of the increasing physico-chemical complexity of organized material groupings, then surely we must lay down a further principle. It is one that is completely consonant with another fact, now universally accepted, that every infinite is characterized by certain effects that are strictly proper to it alone.[2] The principle I mean is that consciousness is the peculiar and specific property of *organized states* of matter; it is a property that cannot be detected, and may therefore be neglected in practice, with low values of complexity, but that gradually emerges and finally becomes dominant, with high values.[3] On the one side you have physics, in the strict sense of the word, which is principally concerned with bringing out the statistical behaviour of extremely simple elements (whose degree of life is therefore

[2]For example, the variation in the mass of bodies moving at extremely high velocities.
[3]This amounts to saying that the behaviour of every cosmic particle may be symbolically represented in our experience as an ellipse constructed with two foci of unequal and varying intensity: F_1, the focus of material arrangement, and F_2, the focus of psychism. F_2 (consciousness) appears initially and increases as a function of F_1 (complexity), but soon shows a persistent tendency to react constructively on F_1 in such a way as to super-complexify it, and at the same time to become, itself, more individualized. In pre-life (the zone of minimal complexities: atoms and molecules) F_2 is imperceptible, and may be regarded as nil. In pre-human life (the zone of complexities of the middle order) F_2 appears, but has still only a slight influence on the growth of F_1, which remains for the most part automatic. Starting with man (the zone of extremely high complexities), F_2, now reflective, takes on to a large extent the function of ensuring the progress of F_1 (through invention), until the latter may be able to free itself by attaining complete autonomy. See below.

infinitely small), handled in extremely large numbers, ranging from the minute to the immense; and on the other side you have a divergent, but connected, branch – biology, which is concerned, in the middle order, with the study of the behaviour and associations of particles which are appreciably interiorized (because extremely complex), and can be considered in isolation. Thus, the two sciences (the science of matter and the science of life) are no longer in opposition, but complementary.

3. This way of looking at things not only introduces order and continuity into our various fields of knowledge, but also makes possible a new and valuable interpretation of the world in which we move. For some time now astronomers have been talking about a universe *expanding in immensity*. Would it not be just as scientific, and even more true, to speak of a universe *involuting in complexity*? Both ways of looking at it (which are perfectly reconcilable) are equally objective and equally free from any unwarranted teleological assumption; but the second of the two would seem to go much further and deeper than the first. For while the explosive expansion of matter in space may well tell us something about the distribution of galaxies and stars, on the other hand a process of complexification and centration of the cosmic stuff upon itself allows us to follow and note, with that stuff's increasing granulation, the correlative rise of interiorization (that is, of psychism) in the world. Moreover, there is every possibility that this simultaneous shift in the organic and the conscious may well be the universe's *one* essential and specific movement.

4. At this first stage in our enquiry, there can as yet be no question of trying to define the *principle* or the particular 'field of force' which causes matter to develop its own complexity in this way (see paragraph 20). On the other hand, it is im-

portant to note the way in which the phenomenon becomes irreversibly more pronounced. First, we have the sub-world of atoms, which are apparently able to develop, each on its own, from nuclear particles, and fall into a limited number of fixed groupings, with no well-defined natural order of sequence from heavy types to light. Then comes the sub-world of molecules, in the most complex forms of which can clearly be seen, if not what we might take to be genealogical descent, at all events chain-structures which suggest the idea of an ontogenesis. Finally, there is the organic sub-world (with its possible sub-divisions), in which the wonderful process of reproduction (and of death . . .) makes it possible for complexification to be continued *additively* from individual to individual, throughout almost indefinitely prolonged phyla.[4] In a word, once the cosmic involution of complexification has been started it cannot stop: on the contrary, in spite of the improbabilities it entails and accumulates, it appears to continue with an infallibility and a constancy which one can only compare (paradoxically) with the inexorable (and *probably allied*) dissipation of matter and energy we find at the other end of things: the latter, the dissipation or de-volution, being a loss in an imperceptible radiation produced by exteriorization, while the former, the involution, is a sublimation produced by synthesis in spirit.

5. All this leads up to the following conclusion: there is a persistent and widespread preconception that life, which appears in the universe as something so fragile and so rare,

---

[4] It is the progress of these 'additions' which defines *true* time or biological time. It should be noted that, in this way, the *body* of each living entity does not act as a containing limit to the latter within the universe (every cosmic particle, be it the smallest electron, is strictly co-extensive with the totality of space and time): the body is only the expression of the living entity's interiority and 'centricity'.

represents no more than a chance accident, and therefore a completely secondary element in cosmogenesis. The hypothesis of 'an involuting world' obviously means that this view must be reversed. Structural necessity demands, in such a world, that the vitalized portion of matter – however weak and localized it may appear – can by no means be regarded as an anomaly, nor as a subsidiary occurrence (nor, to use words one still hears, a mould or fungus); on the contrary, it corresponds to the most central and most solid axis (or, one might say, the very 'apex') of the cosmic 'vortex'. So true is this, that at every point in space-time, whatever its curvature and confines may be, we have to see life – and therefore thought itself – as a force which is everywhere and at all times contained under pressure – and which, accordingly, is only waiting for a favourable opportunity to emerge: and once emerged, to carry its constructive processes (and, with them, its interiorization) right through to the end.

This is what we have to see and accept once and for all: and unless we do this first, we shall never be able to understand anything either about the universe or about what is for us the universe's most advanced expression, the phenomenon of man.

2. *Elementary hominization, or the breakthrough into reflection*

6. However subject to direction the organic involution of the world may be along its general axis of progress, the very nature of the multiple upon which it operates is such that the involution can advance only by endlessly feeling its way. This explains why it is that when we look back and observe the wake it has left behind it in terrestrial biogenesis, we do not see a

well-defined line but one that is broken up into a large number of divergent branches: the countless phyla along which attempts have been made to find those directions which are most favourable for complexity and consciousness. Both from the point of view of 'complexity' and from that of 'consciousness', there has been good reason to wonder whether there were not some objective method of establishing a classification of value between the various filaments of this vast fan-like structure, as yet hardly catalogued by zoologists. After all, by what criterion are we to decide that one particular organic type (with its associated instinct) is more central or higher on the axis of the evolving universe than another? When we look at this spectrum of psychic rays, all of *different shades*, is there any way of recognizing – is it reasonable even to imagine that we may recognize – that some rays exceed the others in absolute value?

We shall answer that there is – provided that due weight be allowed to the phenomenon of *reflection*.

7. Man is the only being, within the limits of our experience, who not only *knows*, but *knows that he knows*.[5] In spite of the unmistakable vastness of the effects of this mental property, it is still inexplicably underestimated by many biologists, who (repeating at this new level a mistake in appreciation made earlier in relation to life – see above, paragraph 5) see in it no more than an exaggeration, or an anomalous form, of the consciousness that is common to all living beings. And yet, whether we try to judge, from the point of view of its physical perfection, the act of reflection itself (a strictly 'punctiform' operation – i.e.

[5] If, as we are sometimes told, other animal species shared this characteristic with us, then those species (which appeared chronologically before man) would long ago have become masters of the world; and in such conditions, man would never have appeared on earth.

a breakthrough at a critical point – effected by a consciousness that is definitively centred upon itself); or whether we concentrate on considering the extraordinary and pre-eminent complexity and co-ordination of the cerebro-nervous systems in which the act becomes possible; or whether, finally and most important of all, we observe the immediate and permanent superiority over the whole of the rest of life obtained by the zoological group in which this mysterious power emerged:[6] in every case an identical, very different and much more constructive conclusion has to be accepted. It may be expressed as follows: at the level of 'reflection', a threshold is crossed or a critical point is passed, and as a result of this something completely new appears – it is as though a *change of state* were produced in consciousness. And the consequence of this is that, however closely attached to other living beings the thinking being may appear to be in its genesis, and in fact is so attached, yet in reality it belongs to a new and higher order, for which we must be careful to reserve a special place in the structure of the world.

8. This prompts the following way of interpreting, in more or less general terms, man's place in nature. Initially (i.e. if we trace it sufficiently far back) the human phylum is (or, to put it more correctly, would appear to be) simply *one among* the thousands of thousands of *other* rays (each one of which is coloured by a particular shade of consciousness and way of knowing) along which the constructive effort of biological evolution is dispersed, as though it were determined to leave no possible road untried. And yet – as subsequent events make clear – there was already something, whether in its temporo-

[6]It is no exaggeration to say that the appearance of thought completely renewed the face of the earth.

spatial situation in the biosphere or in the particular make-up of its cellular elements and its anatomy (the mammals and primates) which was to give this particular phylum a specially favoured place in the race towards higher forms of complexity. In every other direction, the rest of the rays either found their progress halted or were completely refracted in their line of advance, so that it became impossible for them to emerge; meanwhile, this one phylum alone was able, at a given moment (towards the end of the Tertiary period) to break through the mysterious surface which separates the sphere of intelligence from that of instinct: and from that moment (this is what it is essential to understand clearly) the whole of life's main effort forces its way at that one point of breakthrough and spreads out into a whole new compartment of the universe. From a strictly experiential point of view, let me emphasize again, man is originally no more than just one of the cosmic stuff's innumerable attempts to involute upon itself: but because this attempt is the one that succeeded, it is literally true that, starting with that successful attempt,[7] one more animate envelope (a point to which we shall return later) began gradually to extend over the globe, on top of the biosphere.

9. This means that we must add a corollary, clarifying our ideas upon an important point. Today it is accepted finally and without question that, while our science of matter may be, or may be tending to become, a single science, there are in reality several physics. There is the physics of the extremely small, which is different from that which covers the middle order, which again is different from that of the extremely large. That being so, is it not obvious that there must necessarily, and symmetrically, be exactly the same sort of division for the

[7]That is, from the narrowly specialized physiology and psychology of a primate.

173

sciences of life? We still speak of *a single* biology, as though the properties to be observed in organic matter remained the same from the minute to the immense in the scale of complexity. Yet nothing is theoretically more improbable; and in fact nothing is more false or more unproductive than this assumed uniformity of evolutionary laws and forms at every rung of the zoological ladder. In reality, as we are coming to accept, there is probably at the very bottom a biology of viruses and genes, quite distinct from that of cellular beings. And in any case, what is quite certain (even though there is still some reluctance to accept the evidence) is that it is becoming essential to distinguish at the other end, at the very top, a special biology of man: a biology that is necessitated by, and defined by, the breakthrough of reflection. The fact is that three associated factors invade the human phenomenon at the same time as thought: the first is the power of rational invention, by which, as we shall see (paragraph 15), evolution acts as its own springboard; the second is pre-awareness of the future, which presents life with the double problem of death and action; and finally the third is attribution of value to the individual, who moves from being a mere link in the phyletic chain, to the dignity of an element capable of being integrated in an organic totalization.

With this group of allied properties, we are evidently, without leaving life behind, entering into a zone of the universe which science cannot represent: unless, that is, we finally make up our minds to adopt a 'non-Euclidean' geo- (or bio-)metry, if I may put it so, for complexes of an extremely high order – in other words, unless we adopt a biology of n new dimensions.

3. *Collective humanization, or the advance into super-reflection*

10. All that we have said so far may be summed up in the two following propositions, which we have to accept, not as a random choice, but in order to ensure clarity and coherence:

a. The essential phenomenon in the material world is life (because life is interiorized).

b. The essential phenomenon in the living world is man (because man is reflective).

A third step has still to be taken if we are to follow the curve of cosmic involution we have thus sketched in, and carry it through to its end: and this is to make up our minds, as we have solid reasons for doing, to accept this third proposition:

c. The essential phenomenon in the world of man is the gradual totalization of mankind (in which individuals super-reflect upon themselves).

This is the ultimate (or, more correctly, penultimate – see paragraph 24) choice, which will be decisive in determining, at this juncture, our theoretical and practical attitude to war and peace – to effort and resignation – but a choice the soundness of which can be established only by examining, both in history and in the world around us, the mechanism, the effects and, in consequence, the underlying nature, of socialization.

11. Among animals (and this is a point to which we shall shortly have to return) what we call socialization is in itself no more than the manifestation, at the level of highly individualized elements, of those chain-building forces which constantly and universally tend to bring together and interlink the elementary particles (atoms, molecules, cells) of the universe. The only difference is that at these high levels of com-

plexity (at which the effects of disintegration and repulsion are exaggerated), if the organic process of grouping is to be effected appreciably, it requires the presence in the bodies subject to its action of special and rarely encountered properties: such, for example, as the extraordinary aptitude for developing their own mechanism which we see in insects, and (even more strikingly) the wonderful power of linked association which man acquires from his collective immersion in a reflective medium.

Let us concentrate on this last instance, as being the most characteristic and the most to the point for the study and understanding of the phenomenon of synthesis between strongly differentiated and interiorized elements.

12. When, at the beginning of the quaternary period, we first meet the particular group of primates to which we belong, we can still clearly distinguish in it the ramified and divergent structure which is so characteristic of all the other living groups which preceded our own. The fossil men of the Far East (Pithecanthropus, Sinanthropus, Solo Man), it would appear, form a truly independent 'scale', or marginal lamination, which points to the existence elsewhere (in Asia and Africa) of other elements which are more central but still take the form of further scales: this is true, for example, of a 'bulb' of ruminants or of carnivores when it first appears. Very soon, however, certain effects of concentration become apparent above this primitive ramification. At the end of the palaeolithic age, the *sapiens* group, in spite of including numerous leaflets (white, yellow, black) is already forming one single unitary system. Thus a movement of re-involution or convergence emerges and grows more pronounced; and I believe I am right in recognizing in this, as two successive phases occur (one of

expansion, and one of compression), the most essential characteristic of the phenomenon of man.

In the first phase (which covers the neolithic period and the whole of the historical period *right up to the present day*), the socialization of man, being effected from a starting-point in a large number of centres and under only moderate pressure, simply coincided with the gradual occupation of the globe: the reflective layer spread slowly and freely over the non-reflective layer of the earth. There are many who think that we are still living under this elementary system of *crescite et multiplicamini*, of which plurality of nations and states is characteristic. And yet, in the world we know, the expansive movement has already been reversed. After occupying all the free space on the planet, the human wave of socialization has curled back upon itself and is engaged in a process of compenetration and of re-shaping itself which reaches down to its furthest depths (cf. paragraph 16). And it is in the course of this second phase of compression, again initiated at this very time, that the final problems of hominization are coming to the fore, and will sooner or later have to be solved.

13. There can be no doubt whatsoever, we may be sure, about the fact itself, briefly analysed here, of a gradual consolidation and organization of mankind upon itself. On the other hand, when we come to appreciate the value of the phenomenon and to determine its future, it is then that the debate begins and contrary views come into conflict. There are some, we know, for whom 'the individual is everything', and for whom socialization is no more than the by-product of an evolution whose mistake has been to culminate in too great a number of human beings at the same time. Come what may,

this multitude must fall into an orderly pattern; but this completely artificial and superficial arrangement has no longer any connection, we are told, with biology's real structures. Very well: in my view, once again it is precisely this over-cautious and legalistic interpretation of the facts that it is so urgently important to combat. How we can do so, and for what reasons, we may now consider.

As I was saying earlier (paragraph 11), socialization is a direct equivalent, at the level of highly complex elements, of the associations which at a lower level produce the molecules of protein, for example, and the organic tissues; further, and most important of all (paragraph 17), each new and more successful human grouping automatically subtends a further increase of consciousness. There we have two reasons, whose validity is completely objective, I maintain, why the social totalization taking place at this moment can in no way be equated with an accidental and superficial aggregation of living reflective particles. On the other hand, it fits in admirably as a direct continuation of the process from which those particles emerged. Because of an instinctive preconception we have about the slowness of life's movements, we are inclined to believe that hominization has long since come to a halt, and that all it can do in the future is to maintain its present 'ceiling' at our own level; but a close examination of the social phenomenon should open our eyes, and show us that the cosmic involution from which each one of us has emerged has not been arrested. Far from it: it is being continued, with even more vigour than before, in the collective, and at a higher level than our own.[8] 'E pur se muove.'

---

[8] What is more, this collective super-involution has the effect of super-centering each one of us upon our own selves: rightly conducted, totalization personalizes: cf. below.

14. Directly or indirectly, all that follows here will prove to be nothing but a list of the corollaries that result from this identification of human socialization with the main terrestrial axis of evolution. Here we may simply note, for a start, that the mere acceptance of this unflinchingly organic and realist point of view is in itself sufficient (as I have already shown elsewhere[9]) to give a new and most remarkable emphasis to the vicissitudes of man's adventure in the general history of the earth.

a. Zoologically, in the first place, if the *Homo* group is considered from this angle, it forms a perfectly natural picture. Originating, to all appearances, as a mere species or fascicle of species, we find in the end[10] that it is nothing more nor less than a complete phylum (the main growing-point of the tree of life) which is in process of folding back upon itself through all its branches, existing or potential, and on a global scale.

b. Anatomically, in the second place (and this is in full agreement with what modern thought instinctively guesses and anticipates) the social body is seen to be going through a process of organic differentiation – using the word as no metaphor, but in a physical sense – through the development in association of perfectly balanced instruments: collective heredity (or memory) for example, which is transmitted by education or stored in books; mechanization, gradually released from the hand which initiated it, and now extended to planetary dimensions; and, most important of all, progressive cerebralization which is ever more closely and more rapidly bringing together and co-ordinating an ever-increasing number of individual

[9]'The Formation of the Noosphere' in *The Future of Man*, pp. 155ff; Fontana edition, pp. 161ff.
[10]Thereby, too, it goes beyond all the categories of Linnaean classification and all earlier formulations of biological evolution.

insights, and directing them towards ever more clearly defined targets.

c. Finally, physiologically, an unmistakable functional relationship is becoming apparent between these three principal organic instruments (and between many others to which I need not now refer), which throws a great deal of light on the main outlines of the infinitely disturbing chaos of our modern world: the ever more rapid release, as a result of technologically advanced automation, of an increasing quantity of free human energy – a reserve that is now available, and forthwith put to use, to supply fuel for the various forms of research and creation.

And all this, we must realize, is not characteristic of a cyclical system, set up once and for all and automatically turning upon itself: it points to the progressive genesis of what I have called a 'noosphere' – the pan-terrestrial organism in which, by compression and arrangement of the thinking particles, a resurgence of evolution (itself now become reflective) is striving to carry the stuff of the universe towards the higher conditions of a planetary super-reflection. The course it follows in so doing is what we must now analyse: for if it is true that as a result of socialization mankind is continuing to advance towards the highest degree of consciousness, then, at the present rate of acceleration, how unimaginably enormous are the distances to which we shall have travelled after some hundreds of thousands of years.

4. *The orientation of the future, and Omega Point*

15. So: during a first phase of evolution, we have the more or less automatic genesis of man; and in a second phase, the re-

bound of evolution and its extension by means of the devices man's collective imagination has developed.

If only we take the trouble to consider the full implications of the countless events and portents we are now witnessing in the domain of physics, biology and psychology, the evidence we find forces us to this conclusion: that as a result of mankind's now standing upon its own feet, life is here and now entering into a new era of autonomous control and self-orientation. As a direct result of his socialization, man is beginning, with rational design, to take over the biological motive forces which determine his growth – in other words, he is becoming capable of modifying, or even of creating, his own self. Once this has been understood and accepted, can we then foresee the general directions in which the noosphere will tomorrow decide to advance? Or, since reflection entails freedom, must we conclude that when evolution becomes hominized (that is to say, when it acquires a power of auto-direction) it thereby tends simultaneously, and in virtue of its structure, to make it impossible for us to foresee how it will develop? To my mind, there can be no doubt about the answer to that question. Although the human myriad is made up of free elements – or, rather, precisely because it is based on such elements – its line of advance is firmly polarized: so much so that, 'provided Heaven grant it life',[11] it cannot fail, by a sort of statistical infallibility, to carry itself on in a pattern defined by the following properties: constantly increasing unification, centration,

[11]This presupposes, among other favourable conditions, (a) the absence, in the course of anthropogenesis, of any astronomical or biological catastrophe which would destroy the earth or life on earth; (b) the maintenance until the end – or the replacement by synthetic methods – of the natural resources available in the continents, which feed man's individual and social body; (c) effective control, both in quantity and quality, of reproduction in order to avoid over-population of the earth or its invasion by a less satisfactory ethnic group.

and spiritualization – the whole system rising unmistakably towards a critical point of final convergence.

16. *Unification.* This is the immediate and inevitable result of the properties specific to the substance of man when it is subject to the action of two antagonistic, and essentially irresistible, forces: on the one hand, the increase of human population, and, on the other, the restricted surface-area of the earth. It is because of this double planetary condition (demographic expansion in a closed container) that the social phenomenon, as I pointed out earlier, has just entered a final phase of compression. Now – and this is the point that matters – collective man can survive this increasing compression, from which there is no escape, only by developing an ever higher degree of self-arrangement (which means self-organization) in his own structure.[12] And in consequence, while still leaving the road open to the later, 'attractive' action (cf. paragraph 21) of other factors (operating not *a tergo* but *ab ante*) which make for unanimity, he is forced by reasons that are cosmic in scale and urgency gradually to transcend, in his interests and in what he makes, every limit, every frontier, be it political or economic, or even, up to a point, spiritual. One may, indeed, say without any hesitation, as I have already often said, that under a planetary pressure that can only increase with the passage of time,[13] it would be easier to halt the revolution of the earth than it would be to prevent the totalization of mankind.[14]

[12]And this has the further remarkable result that while every advance in organization brings a temporary relief of pressure, it makes every new increase in planetary constriction more noticeable and more rapidly transmitted in man's environment.

[13]Unless we accept the possibility of a drop in pressure by means of 'astronautics'; but this would not, I think, alter the general trend of the phenomenon.

[14]We often meet the idea that totalization means the immobilization (in other words, the death) of mankind. This is completely untrue. Two sorts of movements at least may be envisaged within a unified mankind: surface movements, which result from exchanges of thought between different zones of the noosphere, and movements in

17. *Centration* (in other words, *intensification of consciousness*). A full understanding of the fundamental cosmic relationship between complexity and consciousness will make it plain that this second axis of the future is in fact integral with the first, of which it is simply the continuation or consequence. We have just seen that mankind is being forced by planetary pressure (fortunately, indeed) into a self-organization that is ever more tightly knit around itself. The mechanism and properties, moreover, of vital involution demand that a correlative effort of internal centration shall inevitably correspond to this external imposed centralization.[15] There is thus a sequence of invisibly linked effects by which the more the concentration of the human mass entails its organic arrangement, the more it continually raises the psychic temperature of the noosphere. Nor, so far as I know, is there anything which seems to be able to modify the operation of this law, for as long as the earth is still inhabited or habitable.

18. *Spiritualization.* By this I mean the increasing predominance in the human layer of the reflective (or 'thought') over automatic reactions and instinct. Earlier (p. 167, n. 3) I was saying that every natural unit produced by cosmic involution can be represented symbolically by an ellipse drawn around two allied foci: one, F_1, of material and technological arrangement; the other, F_2, of consciousness (this latter appearing only at the level of life). What it is essential to understand in the case of man, is that once the breakthrough into reflection has

depth, caused by the continual emergence (and kept continually in equilibrium by convergence) of new potential branches at the core of the human mass as it folds back upon itself.

[15]Collective centration, through development of a common vision (cf. paragraph 19); but individual super-centration, too, as a result of totalization (cf. above, p. 178, n. 8).

been made,[16] the biological process of evolution seems to concentrate and to reduce itself more and more (as a result of collective involution) to ensuring the predominance of F2 over F1. The more intensely mankind becomes organized and technologically centred upon itself, the more (in spite of apparent evidence to the contrary) does its upward impulse (its passion for discovery, for knowledge and creation) tend to predominate over its elementary need to establish itself and survive. Thus, it is ultimately by using this index or parameter of the growing autonomy of F2 that we may hope most accurately to extrapolate the curve of hominization to its term.

19. When we try to examine scientifically what sort of end awaits mankind on earth, I would rather there were less talk of catastrophe (that is a gratuitous and lazy hypothesis), or decay (for we have no reason to believe that the noosphere may not be immune from the ravages of old age: the evidence – cf. below – is very much the other way), or of astronautic emigration (an escape that is astronomically improbable). On the contrary, we should, I think, look at the problem both more closely and more deeply, and then make up our minds to draw the final consequences from this essential fact: that noogenesis (which is what anthropogenesis essentially amounts to) is a convergent phenomenon. In other words it is, by its nature, directed towards an ending and a completion that are *internal in origin*. And here I can only repeat, pushing its conclusions as far as they can be taken, what has been the constant theme running through all that I have already said. If it is true, as I hope I have shown, that the human social phenomenon is simply the higher form assumed on earth by the involution

---

[16]By which the conscious, now decisively isolated and individualized, begins distinctly to react, through invention, on its organic support.

of the cosmic stuff upon itself, then we must accept a conclusion
for which the road has been prepared by the emergence
(already adumbrated in the sciences) of a *Weltanschauung*
common to the consciousness of all mankind.[17] By this I mean
that we must recognize the rapidly increasing probability that
we are approaching a *critical point of maturity*, at which man,
now completely reflecting upon himself not only individually
but collectively, will have reached, along the complexity axis
(and this with the full force of his spiritual impact), the extreme
limit of the world. And it is then, if we wish to attribute a
significant direction to our experience and see where it leads,
that it seems we are obliged to envisage in that direction, finally
to round off the phenomenon, the ultimate emergence of
thought on earth into what I have called Omega Point.

20. I shall continue here to use the term 'Omega Point' in
the sense I have long attributed to it: an ultimate and self-
subsistent pole of consciousness, so involved in the world as to
be able to gather into itself, by union, the cosmic elements that
have been brought by technical arrangement to the extreme
limit of their centration – and yet, by reason of its supra-
evolutive (that is to say, transcendent) nature, enabled to be
immune from that fatal regression which is, structurally, a
threat to every edifice whose stuff exists in space and time. In
itself, and by definition, such a centre is not directly apprehen-
sible by us. Yet, even if its presence and its influence cannot be
immediately perceived, there are at least three decisive reasons
why its existence must inevitably, it would appear, be postulated.

a. First and foremost, a reason derived from *irreversibility*.

[17]By this we must understand a vision of the world in which passion plays as large a
part as intellect, a vision glowing with the magical nimbus of all that art and poetry
have gradually accumulated.

From what we have already said, it must follow that once the process of cosmic complexification has been initiated it cannot be halted. Further, at the level of, and starting with, the psychic point of reflection, this *external, relative* irreversibility begins to be duplicated by another irreversibility, which in this case is *internal* and *absolute*. Man becomes aware simultaneously of his power to foresee the future and to invent; and it becomes increasingly clear to him that he would be out of his mind to lend himself to the prolongation of evolution, and still more to its rebound with himself as spring-board, if the irreplaceable and incommunicable essence, both of each individual person and of planetized mankind, were not finally gathered up and integrated into some fulfilment – a fulfilment that would be *for all time*.[18] In other words, in a universe which has become conscious of a future, cosmic involution would immediately come to a halt, checked from within, when confronted by the hopeless prospect of a possible total death. This can mean but one thing: that at that inevitable moment, which must arrive in every thinking being or system sooner or later, when focus F_1 of complexity is about to collapse, a common, supreme, focus must be ready and at hand, in which the F_2s of consciousness can find support and can combine, so that the human ellipse may be redrawn: and this time, with no possibility of collapse.

b. But there is a second reason, too, derived from *polarity*. Up to this point we have been satisfied to note, without explaining, the irresistible character of the movement which causes 'matter' to fold back upon itself. It is, one would say, as though the universe were *falling* along its axis of increasing complexity. The truth is that what is going on is not a fall –

[18] A demand which implies (let there be no mistake about this) no undue self-love: it is a demand based on respect for the value of the 'being'. When enlarged to the scale of the Whole, renunciation ceases to be noble, because it becomes illogical.

for a fall means a passage towards a state of equilibrium: it is, as we noted incidentally, the exact opposite, an arduous climb towards the improbable. – And it is impossible to justify rationally *this inverse form of gravitation*,[19] without conceiving that somewhere, influencing the very heart of the evolutive vortex, there must be a centre which is sufficiently independent and active to cause the totality of the cosmic layer to centre itself (that is, to complexify itself) under the control of, and in the image of, that same independent centre.

c. And finally, there is a reason derived from *unanimity*. One might at first suppose that all that is needed to ensure the formation of the noosphere, to make it 'set', is the action of planetary compression, which forcibly draws together the reflective particles up to the point where it makes them leave their area of increasing mutual repulsion and ultimately causes them to fall within the radius of their mutual attraction. Here again, however (as in the case of 'falling into complexity'), we must beware of over-simple physical analogies drawn from the other extreme of the world, from the domain of the infinitely simple. However compressed the human particles may be, they must ultimately, if they are to group themselves 'centrically', *love* one another – with a love that includes all individuals simultaneously and all as one whole.[20] Yet there is no true love in an atmosphere, however warm it be, of the collective; for the collective is the impersonal. If love is to be born and to become firmly established it must find *an* individualized heart, *an* individualized face. The more closely one examines this

[19]In which the more complex, in spite of its fragility, behaves paradoxically like the more stable . . .
[20]For by nature (or even, one might say, by definition) sympathy is the only energy that can bring beings together centre to centre (which is, incidentally, the only way of ultra-personalizing them).

essential psychic mechanism of union, the more convinced one becomes that the only possible way in which cosmic involution can culminate is to reach its term not simply on a centred *system* of centres, but on *a centre* of centres – that alone, and only that, will suffice.

All these considerations converge and blend and force us to admit that while, in the direction of the immense and the infinitesimal, the world of physics curls back upon itself, or contracts in such a way as hermetically to imprison in itself all the lines of force of the universe – on the other hand, if we follow the axis of complexities, we cannot conceive of thought as attaining the fullness of its culmination and then either halting or falling back upon itself: when thought has reached that peak of intensity it must succeed, somehow, as a result of hyper-centration, in breaking through the temporo-spatial membrane of the phenomenon – until it joins up with a supremely personal, supremely personalizing, being.

II. THE CHRISTIAN PHENOMENON

21. A planetary compression[21] which forces the human mass to organize itself – and that organization releasing an upward spiritual force which finally detaches reflective consciousness from its matrix of technical arrangements, and so allies it extra-phenomenally with the partially transcendent focus of cosmic involution: it is thus that we have just seen the development of the linked sequence we know as the phenomenon of man. Further direct progress along that line is impossible. On the other hand we can take a dialectical swing backwards, to consolidate the road we have travelled, and so hope to build up

[21]Ultimately, gravitational in origin.

fresh impetus. And this is how we can do so: it is a principle derived from general experience that every being acts on its environment through the totality of its self. This means, quite simply, that biological lines of force are inevitably established between living elements – intellectual lines of force between thinking elements – and so on. This being so, to admit, even as a conjecture, the existence at the summit of the universe of an Omega Point, is *ipso facto* to introduce the possibility that certain influences, a certain radiation, psychic in nature, are active around us; and these point to and confirm (under certain conditions, and up to a certain degree) the existence we have postulated, at a higher level than our own persons, of an ultra-pole of personal energy. – And so it is that the significance and importance of the Christian phenomenon become apparent.

22. The Christian phenomenon, historically speaking, is simply the final and central form assumed, following a long and complex phylogenesis, by the persistent emergence at the heart of hominization of the need to worship: and so, by the Christian phenomenon I mean the experiential existence within mankind of a religious current which is characterized by the following group of properties: intense vitality; unusual adaptability, which allows it, unlike other religions, to develop most successfully and chiefly in the noosphere's very area of growth;[22] and finally a remarkable similarity in its dogmatic views (convergence of the universe upon a self-subsistent and suprapersonal God) with all that we have learnt from our study of the phenomenon of man. These various peculiarities might well escape the notice of an uninformed mind, but they awake in the sensitive observer a suspicion that amounts to a certainty.

[22]In what botanists call the meristem.

Is it not reasonable to see in the gradual formation, at the very quick of man's consciousness, of an ever more perfect and more fully developed image of God, just that influence and radiation we were expecting of Omega, reflecting, *revealing*, itself, affectively and intelligibly on the reflective surface of the noosphere? Let us accept this hypothesis; or, better still, let us adhere to this faith.[23] It is apparent that, with that acceptance or adherence, many things that characterize the structure and general progress of the universe are clarified and come into sharper focus.

23. In the first place, the immediate result of this perception of the divine reflection on the world is an important (and, indeed, an essential)[24] confirmation of the *existence* of Omega. But, what is more (through that controlled fertilization of human thought in which Revelation is psycho-experientially expressed for us), all sorts of concrete determinant properties, of very great value both in theory and in practice, become apparent. These relate to the *essence* of Omega (trinitarian nature, for example), and more particularly to its *modes of operation*.

24. If we left out any contribution or support from Revelation, the only conclusion we could deduce from the existence, once that is accepted, of Omega is that the tide of consciousness of which we form a part is not produced simply by some impulse that originates in ourselves. It feels the pull of a star,

[23]This is not the place to analyse the mechanism, but only to determine the dialectical position, of the mysterious 'act of faith' within which the elementary human centre and the divine Megacentre attain a vital *recognition of one another* – starting from, but going beyond, certain signs.

[24]'Essential' on two grounds: first, of course, in a religious sense, to strengthen our worship; but in an intellectual sense also, to assure us that we are right to trust our reason. For if there were no confirmation of the existence of the Omega whom we have recognized as theoretically necessary for the coherence of the world, it would seriously impair our confidence in the constructive value of human reason.

upon which, individually and as one whole, we are completing in union our process of self-interiorization. The layers of the world around us take on a vastly richer and more penetrating radiance when they are seen in the context of a Christic-type creation (one, that is, in which a divine involution steps down to combine with the mounting evolution of the cosmos). I shall have more to say later about the metaphysical concords and mystical consequences of such a vision. From a phenomenal point of view, we may confine ourselves to noting here the relationship which it brings out between what I referred to earlier as 'the critical point of human maturation' on the one hand, and on the other hand the *parousia-point* (or the second coming of Christ in triumph) which at the end of all time rings down the curtain on the Christian horizon. By structural necessity, the two points inevitably coincide – in this sense, that the fulfilment of hominization by ultra-reflection is seen to be a necessary[25] pre-condition of its 'divinization'. And so we see an additional element beginning to take shape in the actual nucleus of the cone of cosmic involution. At first we had recognized that the central phenomenon in the universe is life: in life it is thought, and in thought the collective arrangement of all thoughts in inter-relation to one another. We are now faced by a *fourth choice*, and it brings us to the conclusion that at a still deeper level, at the very heart, that is to say, of the social phenomenon, a sort of *ultra-socialization* is in progress. It is the process by which 'the Church' is gradually formed, its influence animating and assembling in their most sublime form all the spiritual energies of the noosphere: the Church, the reflexively Christified portion of the world – the Church, the

[25]Necessary, but not sufficient. In all this there is, of course, no 'millenniarism', since the point of human ultra-reflection (corresponding to the parousia-point) marks a phase not of rest but of *maximum tension*.

principal focus-point at which inter-human affinities come together through super-charity (cf. paragraph 38) – the Church, the central axis of universal convergence, and the exact meeting-point that springs up between the universe and Omega Point.

2. Metaphysics

25. In the course of the preceding pages I have concentrated solely on disclosing, and tracing to its end, a tangible thread in the world, a *law of recurrence* (cosmic involution), while realizing that its final extrapolation must be checked by a critical reference to a deeper form of experience (perception of the Christic influence). In this second part I shall try to reconstruct deductively (that is, a priori) the system observed in the way I have described, including its theological or revealed extensions, and starting from certain general principles which I take as an absolute. I am fully aware, of course, of the precarious and provisional nature of such a metaphysics; but I know too that it is by such attempts that little by little, proceeding from one approximation to another, we gradually build up both in science and in philosophy the *universe-of-thought* around which, as we have seen, human reflection must one day succeed in coalescing.[26]

26. In classical metaphysics it has always been customary to deduce the world from a starting-point in the notion of *being*, regarded as irreducibly primordial. The most recent investigations of the physicists have shown that the 'common-sense'

[26]The tentative nature of this enquiry, emphasized by Père Teilhard, should be borne in mind. In every domain, and particularly in those he covers, science and reflection can only feel their way. Any judgement of such an essay as this implies and presupposes that the reader shares its approach, which is common to all that Père Teilhard wrote. (Ed.)

evidence which underlies the whole of the *philosophia perennis* is misleading: motion is not independent of the moving body – on the contrary, the moving body is physically engendered by the motion which animates it. Relying on this new principle, I shall try in what follows to show that a line of argument richer and more flexible than the earlier becomes possible if our initial proposition is that being does not represent a final notion, standing in isolation, but is in reality definable (genetically, at least, if not ontologically) by a particular movement which is indissolubly associated with it – that of *union*. Thus one may use the following equations, as the case demands:

to be = to unite oneself, or to unite others (the active form)

to be = to be united and unified by another (the passive form).[27]

Let us, then, note and briefly analyse the successive *phases* of this *metaphysics of union*.[28]

27. In a *first phase*, we have to assume as a prime datum (and in so doing we coincide with classical philosophy) the irreversible and self-sufficient presence of a 'First Being' (our Omega Point). Otherwise it is impossible (both logically and ontologically) to get any purchase – that is, to take a single step forward. But if this initial and final centre is to subsist upon

---

[27]Or, more clearly, in Latin:

Plus esse = plus plura unire (active form)

Plus esse = plus a pluribus uniri (passive form)

Note: in the first expression, it is evident that *'plus plura unire'* does not hold good for God in the case of trinitization, but it exactly fits pleromization (or creation, cf. paragraph 29).*

*To be more = more fully to unite more elements

To be more = to be more fully united from more elements (Ed.)

[28]Here Père Teilhard returns to and develops more fully (by including in it the mystery of God himself) an intuition which first asserted itself in his mind as early as 1917, and which, in one form or another, was to be with him throughout his life. Cf. 'Creative Union' in *Writings in Time of War*, pp. 151–76. (Ed.)

itself in its splendid isolation, then (in conformity with the 'revealed' datum – *phase two*) we are obliged to represent it to ourselves as, in its triune nature, containing its own self-opposition. Thus, even in these primordial depths, the onto-logical principle we adopted as the foundation of our metaphysics is seen to be valid and illuminating: in a sense that is strictly true, God exists only by *uniting himself*. – Let us see how, in another sense, he fulfils himself only *by uniting*.[29]

28. In the very act by which his reality asserts itself, God (we have just seen) makes himself triune. But, what is more, by the very fact that he unifies himself upon himself in order that he may exist, the First Being *ipso facto* stimulates the out-break of another type of opposition, not in the core of his being but at the very opposite pole from himself (*phase three*). The self-subsistent unity, at the pole of being: and as a necessary consequence, surrounding it on the circumference, the multiple – the *pure* multiple (with full emphasis on *pure*), or creatable *nil*, which is nothing – and which nevertheless, by passive potentiality of arrangement (that is to say, of union), is a possibility of being, a prayer for being: a prayer (and here we are in such deep waters that our minds are completely unable to distinguish supreme necessity from supreme freedom)[30]

[29]It will be noticed that here Père Teilhard starts from what is normally the final point in his line of thought – Omega. The elements of this initial assumption are fully analysed in the fourth phase of his 'dialectic of spirit', written a little earlier than this essay. (Cf. *Activation of Energy*, Collins, London, 1970, and Harcourt Brace Jovanovich, New York, 1971, pp. 148–51.) Here he shows how one can envisage Alpha if one starts from Omega. (Ed.)

[30]Except by recognizing the presence of the Free by the infallible sign of an associated love. Similarly, it is love (cf. below, p. 201, n. 43) which makes it possible to distinguish the Eastern 'ineffable of relaxation' from the Christian 'ineffable of tension' (as found, for example, in St John of the Cross).

which it is just as though God had been unable to resist.[31]

29. In classical philosophy (or theology) the Creation, or Participation (which constitutes *phase four*) always tends to be presented as an almost arbitrary act on the part of the first cause, operating (by a causality that is analogically 'efficient') through a completely indeterminate mechanism: an 'act of God', indeed, in the catastrophic sense of the term. In a metaphysics of union, however, while the self-sufficiency and self-determination of the absolute being are retained intact (since, let me again emphasize, the pure multiple at the opposite pole is merely potentiality and pure passivity),[32] on the other hand the creative act takes on a very clearly defined significance and structure. Being, in some way, the fruit of a reflection of God, no longer in God but outside him, the pleromization (as St Paul would have called it) – that is to say, the realization of participated being through arrangement and totalization – emerges as a sort of echo or symmetrical response to Trinitization. It somehow fills a gap; it fits in. And at the same time it

---

[31]Here Teilhard raises the problem of the Creation in its aspect of, while yet without being, existing for God in the form of a 'possible' of which God wishes to have need. Granted the way in which Teilhard thinks of reality, this possible has in some way the already positive and yet completely evanescent appearance of the pure multiple. He calls it 'creatable *nil*' because it is already the stuff in which the universe will be fashioned by process of arrangement and creative union.

In dealing with the freedom of this creative act, Teilhard attains a profound depth of expression here (paragraph 28) and in the accompanying note. As early as 1924 he had written on the same lines: 'God and the world – the Pleroma – the mysterious reality of which we cannot say that it is more beautiful than God himself (since God could dispense with the world), but which we cannot, either, consider completely gratuitous, completely subsidiary, without making Creation unintelligible, the Passion of Christ meaningless, and our own effort completely without value.' (Cf. 'My Universe' in *Science and Christ*, p. 85.)

A metaphysics of union, culminating in the figure of the universal Christ, as Père Teilhard says in paragraph 38 below, gives us some idea of how the creatable *nil* (that is, the world made for Christ, even before it is world) enters on its appointed role in the form of a prayer for being. (Ed.)

[32]Itself only an 'antithetical' reflection of the triune being.

becomes expressible in the same terms as those which served us for our definition of being. To create is to unite.[33]

And this, we shall find, has some remarkable consequences.

a. First, we shall discover that, while Creation can include a limitless number of phases, on the other hand (and in this it somewhat resembles Trinitization) it can be effected only once (if I may use the phrase) 'in God's lifetime'. Indeed, once the reduction of the multiple has been effected, no form of still unsatisfied opposition (either interior or exterior) subsists for the 'pleromized' being. With every conceivable possibility of union (whether active or passive) exhausted, the 'being' has reached the level at which it is saturated.[34]

b. Secondly, we realize that in order to create (for, once again, to create is to unite) God has inevitably to immerse himself in the multiple, so that he may incorporate it in himself.

c. And finally, a much more sensitive point, about which I must now make myself clear – we see that in order to launch an attack on the multiple, God is forced into war with evil, 'the shadow of Creation'.

30. Our ingrained habits of thought are such that we still automatically maintain that the problem of evil is insoluble. And yet, why should this be so? In the old cosmos, which was assumed to have emerged complete from the hands of the Creator, it was only natural to find it difficult to reconcile a partially evil world with the existence of a God who is both good and omnipotent. But with our modern view of a universe

[33]Provided, of course (cf. paragraph 26), that we reject what common sense has so long told us about the real distinction between mover and moved, and so cease to imagine that the act of union can be effected only upon a pre-existing substratum, the 'true' object of creation.

[34]There is obviously an infinite number of conceivable *modalities* for the single universe which is the object of creation: but these various modalities are like a number of different mountain tracks which are bound to lead in the end to the same peak.

in a state of *cosmogenesis* – and more particularly in a state of 'involution' – how can so many well-ordered minds still persist in failing to see that, intellectually[35] speaking, the only too familiar problem *no longer exists*. Leaving behind imaginary speculations, let us consider the real conditions which, we have just seen, must be satisfied by the creative act. Our analysis has led to the conclusion that *not through inability*, but by reason of the *very structure of the nil* to which he stoops, God can proceed to creation *in only one way*: he must arrange, and, under his magnetic influence and using the tentative operation of enormous numbers, gradually unify an immense multitude of elements. Initially, these are infinite in number, extremely simple, and hardly conscious – then they gradually become fewer, more complex, and ultimately endowed with reflection. What, then, is the inevitable counterpart to every success gained in the course of such a process, if not that it has to be paid for by a certain amount of wastage? So we find physical discords or decompositions in the pre-living; suffering in the living; sin in the domain of freedom. There can be no *order in process of formation* which does not at every stage imply *some disorder*. In this ontological (or, more correctly, ontogenic) condition inherent in the participated, there is nothing which impairs the dignity or limits the omnipotence of the Creator, nothing which in any way smacks of Manichaeanism. In itself, the pure, unorganized Multiple is not evil: but because it is multiple, which means that it is essentially subject in its arrangements to the operation of chance, it is absolutely barred

[35]*Intellectually* as opposed to *vitally*. It is obviously one thing to explain rationally the com-possibility of evil and God, and quite another to have to put up with physical or mental suffering. If, in the former case, a chain of reasoning will serve our purpose, even so we need nothing less than the transforming virtue of what I shall later (paragraph 38) be referring to as 'super-charity' to release us from the latter.

from progressing towards unity without sporadically engendering evil:[36] and that *as a matter of statistical necessity.* '*Necessarium est ut adveniant scandala.*' If (as we must, I believe, inevitably admit) our reason can see only one way in which it is possible for God to create – and that is evolutively, by process of unification – then evil is an inevitable by-product. It appears as a forfeit inseparable from Creation.[37]

31. And so we can see how a series of notions, long regarded as independent, gradually comes to form a linked organic pattern. No God (up to a certain point . . .) without creative union. No creation without incarnational immersion. No incarnation without redemptive repayment.[38] In a metaphysics of union, the three fundamental 'mysteries' of Christianity[39] are seen to be simply the three aspects of one and the same mystery of mysteries, that of pleromization (or unifying reduction of the multiple). And at the same time a re-invigorated Christology stands out as not simply the historical or juridical, but as the structural axis, of the whole of theology. Between the Word on one side, and the Man-Jesus on the other, a sort of 'third Christic nature' (if I may use so bold a phrase) emerges – constantly to be found in the writings of St Paul: it is the nature of the total and totalizing Christ, in whom the individual

[36]However free it may be.

[37]Let me emphasize here the principle which gives us a simple and fruitful interpretation of original sin – the theological necessity of baptism being explained by the genetic solidarity of all mankind (permeated, by statistical necessity, with sin), in which the collective ties which bind individuals are seen to be even more real and more deeply rooted than any strictly and 'lineally' hereditary type of linkage.

[38]We should probably distinguish *two* elements in the 'creative forfeit' expressed by the idea of Redemption: a. First, of course, compensation for statistical disorders; b. but also a specific effort towards unification, overcoming a sort of ontological slope (or inertia) because of which participated being constantly tends to fall back towards multiplicity.

[39]Which, I repeat, have hitherto been commonly represented as entirely separable from one another. In popular teaching, it is still generally accepted that: 1. God could

human element born of Mary is subject to the transforming influence of the Resurrection, and so raised not merely to the state of cosmic element (an element, one might say, of what makes up the whole cosmic milieu or curvature) but to that of ultimate psychic centre of universal concentration.[40]

So there re-appears, at the term of our metaphysics, the same Christic point towards which, as we had already seen, the phenomenon of man seems experientially to be making its way, and on which it seems to converge: – and the same point, too, as we have still to see, around which the very essence of modern mysticism is coming to re-discover and re-shape itself, and so conquer the future.

3. Mysticism

32. What I mean here by mysticism is the need, the science and the art of attaining simultaneously, and each through the other, the universal and the spiritual. To become at the same time, and by the same act, one with All, through release from all multiplicity or material gravity: there you have, deeper than any ambition for pleasure, for wealth or power, the essential dream of the human soul – a dream which, as we shall see, is still incorrectly and incompletely expressed in the

---

absolutely (*simpliciter*) create or not create; 2. If he did create, he could do so with or without the Incarnation; 3. And that if he made himself incarnate, he could do so with or without suffering. Whatever one's attitude, it is this conceptual pluralism, I believe, that must be corrected.

[40]Each element in the universe (cf. p. 169, n. 4) is both physically and metaphysically an elementary centre in relation to the totality of time and space. In Christ, however, this co-extension of co-existence has become co-extension of sovereignty.

noosphere, but can be clearly recognized throughout the already lengthy history of holiness.

33. An effort to escape spiritually, through universalization, into the ineffable: mystics of all religions and of all times[41] are in complete agreement that it is this general direction that must be followed by the interior life as it seeks for perfection. Nevertheless, I have long been convinced that this superficial unanimity disguises a serious opposition (or even a fundamental incompatibility) which originates in a confusion between two symmetrical but 'antipodal' approaches to the understanding, and hence to the pursuit, of spirit.[42]

a. If the first road, which for convenience I shall call 'the road of the East' is followed, spiritual unification is conceived as being effected through return to a common 'divine' basis *underlying*, and *more real than*, all the sensibly perceptible determinants of the universe. From this point of view, mystical unity appears and is acquired by direct suppression of the multiple: that is to say, by relaxing the cosmic effort towards differentiation in ourselves and around ourselves. It is pantheism of identification, the spirit of 'release of tension': unification by co-extension with the sphere through dissolution.

b. If the second road, however, is followed (the road of the West), it is impossible to become one with All unless we carry to their extreme limit, in their direction at once of differentiation and convergence, the dispersed elements which constitute us and surround us. From this second point of view, the

[41]See a selection of quotations from many different sources in Aldous Huxley's *Perennial Philosophy*.
[42]For a fuller analysis of the characteristics of the two roads, see 'The Spiritual Contribution of the Far East' in this volume, and 'How I believe' in *Christianity and Evolution*, pp. 96–132. (Ed.)

'common basis' of the Eastern road is mere illusion: all that exists is a central focus at which we can arrive only by extending to their meeting-point the countless guide-lines of the universe. Pantheism of union (and hence of love): spirit 'of tension'; unification by concentration and hyper-centration at the centre of the sphere.

Surprisingly, it would not appear that a clear distinction has yet been drawn between these two diametrically contrasted attitudes: and this accounts for the confusion which muddles together or identifies the ineffable of the Vedanta and that of, for example, St John of the Cross[43] – and so not only allows any number of excellent souls to become helpless victims of the most pernicious illusions produced in the East, but also (what is more serious) delays a task that is daily becoming more urgent – the individualization and the full flowering of a valid and powerful modern mysticism.

34. In this connection, the first point – and it is the decisive point – to bring out and fix in our minds is this: once our physics and metaphysics have been accepted, as expressed in the terms we agreed on earlier, then there can be no possible hesitation about the direction we must choose at this crossroads. In a universe of self-involution, the only homogeneous form of spiritualization, the only viable mysticism, must be – what, in fact, they are becoming more and more – a positive act not of relaxation, but of active convergence and concentration.

[43]When approached by the road of the East (identification) the ineffable is not such that it can be loved. By the road of the West (union) it is attained through a continuation of the direction of love. This very simple criterion makes it possible to distinguish and keep separate, as being antithetical, verbal expressions that are almost identical when used by Christian or Hindu. Cf. above, p. 194, n. 30.

Now that we have realized this, let us try to define and describe the two modes – one simply rational, the other specifically Christian – in which the human swarm, by an instinctive and imperative choice, is adopting the road of the West: a mass movement which we can even now witness for ourselves.

35. At the psychological root of all mysticism there lies, if I am not mistaken, the more or less ill-defined need or magnetic power which urges each conscious element to become united with the surrounding whole. This *cosmic* sense is undoubtedly akin to and as primordial as the sense of sex; we find it sporadically very much alive in some poets or visionaries, but it has hitherto remained dormant, or at any rate localized (in an elementary and questionable form) in a number of Eastern centres. In recent times there has emerged in our interior vision a universe that has at last become knit together around itself and around us, in its passage through the immensity of time and space. As a result of this, it is quite evident that the passionate awareness of a universal quasi-presence is tending to be aroused, to become correctly adjusted and to be generalized in human consciousness. The sense of evolution, the sense of species, the sense of the earth, the sense of man: these are so many different and preliminary expressions of one and the same thirst for unification – and, it goes without saying, they all, by establishing a correct relation to the object that gives rise to them and stimulates them, conform to the Western type of spiritualization and worship. Contradicting the most obstinate of preconceived opinions, the light is on the point of appearing not from the East, but here at home, in the very heart of technology and research.

36. From this point of view, it is in the direction of a dynamic and progressive neo-humanism (one, that is, which

is based on man's having become conscious of being the responsible axis of cosmic evolution) that a mysticism of tomorrow is beginning to assert itself as the answer to the new and constantly increasing needs of anthropogenesis. A common faith in a future of the earth is a frame of mind, perhaps even the only frame of mind, that can create the psychic atmosphere required for a spiritual convergence of all human consciousness: but can that common faith, in its merely natural form, constitute a religion that will be permanently satisfactory? . . . In other words, is not *something more* required to maintain the evolutive effort of hominization unimpaired and unfaltering to its final term, and to love it: does it not call for the manifest appearance and explicit intervention of the ultimate focus of biological involution? I believe that it does; and it is here that Christic faith comes in to take over from and to consummate faith in man.

37. Twice already we have met this supreme crown to both the phenomenon of man and the metaphysics of union – the mysterious figure of the parousiac or risen Christ, in whom the two linked processes of involution and pleromization are simultaneously consummated. In 'Christ-Omega', the universal comes into exact focus and assumes a personal form. Biologically and ontologically speaking, there is nothing more consistent, and at the same time nothing bolder,[44] than this identification we envisage, at the upper limits of noogenesis, between the apparently contradictory properties of the whole and the element. And it follows necessarily that, psychologically, there is nothing more miraculously fruitful, because, in this antici-

[44]Left to itself, biology would no doubt shrink from carrying the effects of socialization beyond a common reflection (unanimity), which combines and interlocks the thinking elements in a sort of vaulting – but without the appearance of a centre of common consciousness.

pated centre to the total sphere, attitudes and 'passions' are able to meet and to be multiplied by one another, which in every other mental compass remain irreparably separate. 'To lose oneself in the cosmic'; 'to believe in and devote oneself to progress'; 'to love another being of the same sort as one's self'; such are the only relationships possible in a purely human ambience – and there they cannot but be independent of one another or even mutually exclusive. 'To love (with real love, with a true love) the universe in process of formation, in its totality and in its details', 'to love evolution' – that is the paradoxical interior act that can immediately be effected in the Christic ambience. For the man who has once thoroughly understood the nature of a world in which cosmogenesis, proceeding along the axis of anthropogenesis, culminates in a Christogenesis – for that man, everything, in every element and event of the universe, is bathed in light and warmth, everything becomes animate and a fit object for love and worship – not, indeed, directly in itself (as popular pantheism would have it) but at a deeper level than itself: that is, at the extreme and unique term of its development.

Once things are seen in this light, it is impossible to adhere to Christ without doing all one can to assist the whole forward drive. In that same light, too, communion becomes an impassioned participation in universal action; and expectation of the parousia merges exactly, as we saw earlier (paragraph 24) with the coming of a maturity of man; and the upward movement towards the 'above' combines harmoniously with the drive 'ahead' ... And from all this follows that Christian charity, generally presented as a mere soothing lotion poured over the world's suffering, is seen to be the most complete and the most active agent of hominization.

By Christian charity, in the first place, the reflected evolutive effort, whether considered in its individual parts or as one whole, is charged, as we have just said, with love: and that is the only way in which the full depths of its whole psychic reserves can be released.

By charity, again, the miseries of failure and vital diminishment – even these! – are transformed into factors of unitive excentration (by which I mean the gift to, and transition into, another greater than self): so that they cease to appear as a waste-product of creation and, by a miracle of spiritual superdynamics, they become a positive factor of super-evolution: the true and supreme solution of the problem of evil (cf. above, p. 197, n. 35).

Thereby, too, if the vast and formidably complex motor of evolution is to drive ahead under full power, without distorting a single working part, Christian mysticism, the higher and personalized form of the mysticism of the West, must be recognized by the thinking mind as the perfect energy for the purpose, the eminently appropriate energy. – And in that conclusion we have a most significant indication that nothing can prevent it from becoming the universal and essential mysticism of tomorrow.

CONCLUSION

38. A phenomenology of involution, leading up to the notion of super-reflection. A metaphysics of union, culminating in the figure of the universal-Christ. A mysticism of centration, summed up in the total and totalizing attitude of a love of evolution. Super-humanity crowned by a super-Christ, him-

self principle of super-charity. Such are the three coherent and complementary aspects under which the organic one-ness of a convergent universe is made manifest to us intellectually, emotionally, and in our practical activity.

Paris, 12 August 1948

APPENDIX

1. *Note to the Phenomenon of Man: on some analogies or hidden relationships between gravity and consciousness*

A remarkable kinship can undoubtedly be detected between two processes, both of which are gradual and irreversible: the 'mass concentration' of matter upon itself as a result of gravity, and its psychic centration as a result of organic involution. Both processes occur only in the immense (the spatially immense, or the immense of complexity). Both tend towards a folding-back upon themselves which is total and universal in order. And finally both constantly support one another in the course of their development (without gravity there would be no large molecules, and no planetization of man).

If, as modern physics seems to accept as a definitive fact, gravity is fundamentally no more than an effect of inertia connected with a *curvature* of space-time, must we not conclude that life, too, behaves, and may be treated by the physicist, as another form of 'inertia': corresponding, in this case, not to an *incurvation*, but to an *interiorization* of the same 'continuum'?

To frame the question is obviously not the same as to answer it. But it is surely one step in that direction to have reduced the two phenomena to the same dimensions and to the same dignity of 'universal cosmic effects'.

2. Note to the Christian Phenomenon: on the 'bi-axial' nature of the Incarnation

So long as the universe was regarded as a static system – which means, in practice, made from a stuff which is genetically amorphous – the coming into it of the kingdom of God raised no structural difficulty. The *plastic* layers of human destiny had simply to adjust themselves around the incarnate Word (to the measure of, and under the control of, the latter). Once, however (and this is what really matters), the universe is defined, as it is today, in terms not of *cosmos* but of *cosmogenesis*, then the problem of the Incarnation becomes more complex: for an adjustment has now to be made between *two* different and partially autonomous *axes*: that of anthropogenesis, and that of Christo-genesis.

Hence the importance, or rather the necessity, of a Christology in which there is a coincidence of the human and the Christic points of planetary maturity and parousia.

3. Note to Metaphysics: on the notion of 'paired' entities

Rather than regarding (as I have done in paragraph 26) *esse* as further definable by *unire* (or *uniri*), it would perhaps be better to take the two notions of *being* and *union* (or, if you like, *moving body* and *motion*) as forming a natural pair, the two terms of which, while each equally primordial and fundamentally irreducible, are nevertheless ontologically inseparable – like the two surfaces of one and the same plane – and constrained to vary simultaneously in the same direction.[45]

The introduction into metaphysics of such *paired entities* (well represented in physics, for example by the pairs mass-velocity, or electricity-magnetism; or in psychology by understanding-love) might well be an important step forward in our thinking. It would mean the end of many unreal problems, which arise from the temptation speciously to isolate, or determine the precedence between, the two terms of each pair. Further, it would open up a new line of thought in approaching the problem of the relationships that hold good inside the most mysterious of all those pairs: *Ens a se* and *participated being*.

Auvergne, Les Moulins, near Neuville, 26 August 1948

[45]This last point being characteristic of what one might call pairs of the *first species*. In other pairs (of the *second species*), spirit-matter (i.e. unity-plurality) for example, the two associated terms vary inversely in relation to one another.

SOME NOTES ON
THE MYSTICAL SENSE:
AN ATTEMPT AT
CLARIFICATION

1. The mystical sense is essentially a feeling for, a presentiment of, the total and final unity of the world, beyond its present sensibly apprehended multiplicity: it is a cosmic sense of 'oneness'.[1] This holds good for the Hindu and the Sufi, no less than for the Christian. It enables us to appreciate the mystical 'tenor' of a piece of literature or of a man's life, but its expression varies greatly according to circumstances.

2. Both a priori and a posteriori, two principal ways (and only two – I wonder?) of realizing oneness suggest themselves and have been tried by mystics. (Two roads, or rather two *components*, that have hitherto to all intents and purposes been merged into one.)

a. The first road: to become one with all by co-extension 'with the sphere': that is to say, by suppression of all internal and external determinants, to come together with a sort of common stuff which *underlies* the variety of concrete beings. Access to Aldous Huxley's 'common ground'.

This procedure leads ultimately to an *identification* of each and all with the common ground – to an ineffable of de-differentiation and de-personalization.

Both by definition and by structure, this is mysticism WITHOUT LOVE.

[1]Here, and later, Père Teilhard uses the English word. (Ed.)

b. The second road: to become one with all by access to the centre of the cosmic sphere, conceived as being in a state of (and possessing the power of) concentration upon itself with time. This access is no longer by 'dissolution' but through a peak of intensity arrived at by what is most incommunicable in each element.

This procedure leads ultimately to an ultra-personalizing, ultra-determining, and ultra-differentiating UNIFICATION of the elements within a *common focus*; the specific effect of LOVE.

In the first case, God (an impersonal 'God') was *all*. In the second, God (an ultra-personal, because 'centric', God) is 'all in all' (which is precisely as St Paul puts it).

3. It would appear that only the second road – a road not yet described in any 'book' (?!) (the 'road of the West', born from the Christianity-modern-world contact) – is the true path 'towards and for' oneness. Only this road of unification

a. respects the facts and history (science and history), which shows us consciousness (spirit) as a process of differentiation and synthesis;

b. and at the same time retains in 'spiritual' man that intensity, that ardour, that 'drive',[2] which are, for us, inseparable from the idea of true mysticism. – The road of tension, not of relaxation.

4. Structurally (theology) and practically (primacy of charity), Christianity follows (*is*) road 2.

At the same time, we have to recognize that, as a result of a certain excess of anthropomorphism (or primitive nationalism) the Judaeo-Christian mystical current has had some difficulty in getting rid of a point of view which sought oneness too

[2]Here again Père Teilhard uses the English word. (Ed.)

exclusively in *singleness*, rather than in God's *synthetic power*. God loved *above* all things (rather than *in* and *through* all things). This accounts for a certain 'lack of richness' in the mysticism of the prophets and of many saints: it is too 'Jewish' or too 'human' in the narrow sense of the words – not sufficiently universalist and cosmic (there are exceptions, of course: Eckhart, Francis of Assisi, St John of the Cross . . .).

5. I need no more than mention one perverted way of seeking oneness:

'suppression of the multiple, in destruction and death, and so leaving only "God" subsisting.'

It is doubtful whether this morbid interpretation has ever fed a true religious and mystical current. But, in as much as it represents a distortion or perversion, it has to be guarded against; for it is a *constant potential danger* (*suffering of annihilation* being confused with *suffering of transformation*). Can we be quite certain that traces of this 'illusion' may not still be found in some interpretations of the meaning of the Cross? . . .

Winter, 1951

A SUMMARY OF MY
'PHENOMENOLOGICAL' VIEW
OF THE WORLD:
THE STARTING-POINT AND KEY
OF THE WHOLE SYSTEM

'DEVELOPING a counter-current that cuts across entropy, there is a cosmic drift of matter towards states of arrangement that show progressively greater centro-complexity (this occurring in the direction of – or within – a "third infinite", the *infinite of complexity*, which is just as real as the infinitesimal or the immense). And consciousness presents itself to our experience as the effect or the *specific* property of this complexity, when the latter is taken to extremely high values.'

If this law of recurrence (I call it the law of 'complexity-consciousness') is applied to the history of the world, we see the emergence of an ascending series of critical points and outstanding developments, which are as follows.

1. *Critical point of vitalization*
Somewhere, at the level of the proteins, an initial emergence of consciousness is produced within the pre-living (at least as far as our experience goes). And, by virtue of the accompanying mechanism of 'reproduction', the rise of complexity on earth increases its pace *phyletically* (the genesis of species, or speciation).

Starting from this stage (and in the case of the higher living beings) it becomes possible to 'measure' the advance of organic complexification by the progress of cerebration. That device enables us to distinguish, within the biosphere, a specially favoured axis of complexity-consciousness: that of the primates.

2. *Critical point of reflection (or hominization)*

As a result of some 'hominizing' cerebral mutation, which appears among the anthropoids towards the end of the Tertiary period, psychic reflection – not simply 'knowing' but 'knowing that one knows' – bursts upon the world and opens up an entirely new domain for evolution. With man (apparently no more than a new zoological 'family') it is in fact a *second species of life* that begins, bringing with it its new cycle of possible patterns of arrangement and its own special planetary envelope (the noosphere).

3. *Development of co-reflection (and rise of an ultra-human)*

If it is applied to the great phenomenon of human socialization, the criterion of complexity-consciousness provides some decisive evidence. On the one hand, an irresistible and irreversible technico-cultural organization, noospheric in dimension, is manifestly in progress of development within human society. On the other hand, as an effect of co-reflection, the human mind is continually rising up collectively – collectively, because of the links forged by technology – to the appreciation of new dimensions: for example, the evolutionary organicity and corpuscular structure of the universe. Here the 'organization-interiorization' pair can again be clearly distinguished. This means that all around us the fundamental process of cosmogenesis is continuing just as before (or even is making a fresh and more vigorous start).[1] Considered as a zoological whole, mankind is presenting the unique spectacle of a phylum that is organico-physically synthesizing upon itself. It is, indeed, a 'corpusculization' and a 'centration' (or centering) upon itself of the noosphere *as a whole*.

4. *Probability of a critical point of ultra-reflection ahead of us*

If it is extrapolated into the future, mankind's technico-mental convergence upon itself forces us to envisage a climax of co-reflection, at some *finite* distance in time ahead of us: for this we can find no better (indeed, no other) definition than a critical point of ultra-reflection. We cannot, of course, either imagine or describe such a phenomenon, which would seem to imply an escape from space and time. Nevertheless there are certain precise conditions in the field of energetics that must be satisfied by the event we anticipate (a more pronounced awakening in man, as the event comes closer, of the 'zest for evolution' and the 'will to live'); and from these we are obliged to conclude that ultra-reflection coincides with a final attainment of irreversibility. This must be so, since the prospect of a total death would be so disheartening as to stop the further development of hominization.

It is to this higher term of human co-reflection (which means, in fact, unanimization) that I have given the name of 'Omega Point': the cosmic, personalizing centre of unification and union.

5. *The likelihood of a reaction (or 'reflection') of Omega on the*

[1] The only difference being that, starting with man, cosmic complexification clearly and unmistakably takes the form no longer of a merely fortuitous arrangement arrived at as a statistical consequence of large numbers – but ultimately, in its most vitally active sections, of a planned self-arrangement.

human in the course of co-reflection (Revelation and the Christian phenomenon)

The more we consider the indispensability of an Omega to maintain and animate the continued progress of hominized evolution, the more clearly we can see two things.

The first is that a purely conjectural Omega – one that was arrived at simply by 'calculation' – would be powerless to keep active in man's heart a passion strong enough to make him continue the process of hominization to the very end.

The second is that if Omega does really exist, it is difficult not to accept that its supreme 'Ego' in some way makes itself felt as such by all the imperfect Egos (that is to say all the reflective elements) of the universe.

From this point of view the ancient and traditional idea of 'Revelation' reappears and finds a place in cosmogenesis – entering it, this time, through biology and the energetics of evolution.

From this point of view, again, the Christian mystical current takes on an extraordinary significance and actuality: and this because, while it is true that, by the logic of energetics, the warmth of some intense faith is absolutely indispensable to the completion of the process of complexity-consciousness, at the same time it is equally true (how true, you have only to look around the world to realize) that at the present moment no faith can be distinguished that is capable of fully taking over (by 'amorizing' it) a convergent cosmogenesis, except faith in a Christ, a Christ of the pleroma and parousia, *in quo omnia constant*, in whom all things find their consistence.[2]

New York, 14 January 1954

[2]Colossians 1: 17.

INDEX

agnosticism, 40, 55, 131
Allegra, Fr G. M., 100, 103n, 105n
Amida Buddha, 136
Andrée, S. A., 122
anthropogenesis, 40, 144, 151, 156n, 158n, 181n, 184, 207; and Christogenesis, 159, 204; new needs, 203
apologetics, 30, 35
Aristotle, 14
art; and human energy, 88-90; threefold function, 89-91
asceticism, 60, 64-5, 75
astronautics, 152, 182n, 184
astrophysics, 152, 182n, 184
atoms, 167n, 169, 175
aviators, first, 21-2, 122, 125

baptism, 198n
being and union, 162, 193, 207
Bhakti Yoga, 139n
Bible, 43n
biogenesis, 156n, 170
biology, 9, 114, 203n; divisions, 174; and physics, 167-8; 'theological', 80
biosphere, 173, 213
Bonansea, Fr B. M., 100, 103n
Bossuet, J.-B., 15, 22
Bouvelles, C. de, 165n
Brahmanism, 43
Buddha, 30, 41, 51
Buddhism, 23, 43, 44-5, 134, 135; and chastity, 60; Chinese, 136; new forms, 47
Buffon, G. L. L., 18

carnivores, 176

cells, 175
centration; collective, 183n; hyper-, 188; of man upon himself, 117-18, 124-5; man's increased, 183, 183n
cephalization, 144
cerebralization, 179-80
Charcot, J.-B., 122
charity, Christian; as active agent of hominization, 204-5; need for readjustment, 31, 33, 96, 100; and progress, 128; replacement by sense of the earth, 95; super-, 197n, 206
chastity, 60, 68, 69, 77, 82, 84; empirical Christian approach, 61-6; and freedom of spirit, 77n; querying of moral value, 66-8, 70-1, 79
China; and primacy of the tangible, 135-6; spiritual contribution, 139-40, 144, 146
Christ; centre of universal convergence, 55; co-extension of sovereignty, 199n; faith in, 25, 203, 215; the King, 98-9; message of, 24n; and the multiple, 58;-Omega, 98, 203; second coming, 153, 154-5, 191; and sense of man, 35, 37-9; significance in evolving world, 11; total, 198; universal, 59, 98-100, 195n, 205
Christian; new type, 12; zeal for creation, 32
Christian phenomenon, 189
Christianity, 23n, 148; ascensional force of, 156, 158; causes of loss of

216